In loving memory of my mother and father

Rosemarie A. Poggi
December 27, 1931 - November 16, 2008

Amleto A. ("Babe") Poggi
November 25, 1926 - November 29, 2016

Contents

Preface	xi

FAMILY FIRST

A Stitch in Time	15
Say My Name	18
Where I'm From	19
My Father, the Veteran	22
Battle Weary	24
Mom's Quotes	25
Blood Sisters	27
Easter Sunday	29
Family Doctor Makes Final House Call	30
A Moment with My Mother	32
Grandmom's Chair	34
At the Dinner Table	36
A Giraffe	38
There, There	39
Happy Birthday, Dear Brother	41
My Life in 100 Words	43
My Date with Dad	44
A Winter Visit with Dad	47

My Father's Hands	50
My Most Memorable Christmas Gift	52
A World of Thanks	54
Morning	55
The Kiss	58
When God Winked	60
When Your Child Graduates College	62
Shopping with My Sister	64
Always Something There to Remind Me	66
Ushered Over with Grace	68
Snowstorm Phone Call	71
I Am That Woman	72

HEART OF THE HOME

The Front Porch	79
The Heart-Attack Couch	82
The Guest Room	85
My Bout with Lyme Disease	87
Firefighters to the Rescue	93
Letter to a Bath	95
Yard Sale to Salvage Yard	97
On a Bicycle Built for Two	99
Kitchen Bouquet	101
Mrs. Fix-It	102
Showering Outdoors	104
Shake the Toilet	106
Flying from the Nest	108
An Artificial Christmas Tree	110
Minimizing with My Sisters	112

FOOD IS LOVE

Biscotti for My Accountant	117
Texas Caviar	119
Top 10 Food Memories	120
Sweet Tooth	122
My First and Last St. Patrick's Day Dinner	123
Easy Pasta Recipe	125
A Lobster Tale	126
Spinach Balls	128
Remembering Angelo	129
The Secret to Making the Best Pizzelle	131

SCHOOL DAYS

First Day of School Pictures	135
Teacher's Helper	136
Wit and Wisdom of Fifth Graders	137
Second Grade Field Trip	139
What I Learned in Wood Shop	141
Home from College	142
Favorite Teachers	143
Villanova Reunion: Touched by a Friend	144
When Your First Love Dies	146

NAMASTE

Feel Good in Tree Pose	153
Intelligent Yoga Feet	155
Pursuit of a Headstand	157
To Pee or Not to Pee	160
Shoveling to a Supported Backbend	161

How Vinyasa Improved My Golf Swing	162
Yoga in the Dentist's Chair	164
Handstand to Hospital	166
Yoga on the Beach	168
Sun Salutation to Sleep	169

TRAVELING AROUND

A Chartreuse Sky	173
The Old Station Wagon	175
A Friendly Walk	177
Farewell, Four-Wheeled Friend	179
Searching for Imperfections	181
Boston's Garden of Remembrance	182
Goodbye, Summer	183

JUST FOR FUN

The Weekend I Didn't Get Engaged	187
So You Didn't Win the Powerball Lottery	191
Hips Don't Lie	192
Is That a Cat?	193
I'm Ready!	196
Part-Time Jobs	197
The Stillness of Summer	198
Where Do You Sit?	199
These Boots Are Made for ... Everything	200
Women's Winning Suits	202
You Don't Ask, You Don't Get	204
Favorite Time of the Week	206

Acknowledgments

Preface

I mused about starting a blog for months but couldn't decide on a title or theme. Then one morning, I went to yoga and positioned my mat near a door. I was in downward dog position halfway through the class when a cool draft swept through and brushed my face. In that moment of clarity, the blog title, *Musing Off the Mat*, came to me.

    I decided to write about everyday things that make me shake my head in wonder: reflections about family life, my home, books, food, yoga, and more. I wrote because I wanted to practice the craft and be accountable to myself. Every Monday (and sometimes more often) for four years, I posted a personal essay or short observation on the blog. Readers responded. They told me they liked knowing that at the beginning of their week, they'd receive a light or thoughtful note from me. This book is a compilation of the most popular stories. I hope you enjoy it.

Family FIRST

A Stitch in Time

My seven-year-old daughter wrote, "I was the servant today" on my fine white linen tablecloth. Proud to have carried the delicate serving dishes from the kitchen into the dining room that Christmas Day, Kristin signed her name and wrote the year under her message. I embroidered her message in green.

Some people record their family history in a journal or letters. My family history is recorded on a tablecloth in pencil then preserved with red and green embroidery over each word—red for odd years and green for even years.

We've recorded events momentous and ordinary, such as our exciting family trip to Italy, the year the Red Sox won the World Series, Gary's broken elbow and—four years later—Melissa's broken elbow, new jobs, and adolescent rites of passage, including getting braces, pierced ears, and driver's licenses. The tablecloth documents several extended family member milestones such as the year my niece Holly survived brain surgery and wrote, "Miracles Happen." Sad events have been noted as well: my mother's passing, and when "The world changed on September 11, 2001."

When I reach for the tablecloth in my linen closet the week before Christmas, it's like unwrapping a treasure. I still get a thrill of anticipation when I gingerly unfold it. Then I set the table in the dining room, creating a festive and nostalgic mood for my family. I spread the ironed cloth over the table pads, running my hands over the words of love while smoothing it out. Then I adorn it with my fine Lenox china and an elegant centerpiece.

With the dining table set, my husband, daughters, and I circle the gathering place to peruse the memories of years past. I particularly enjoy seeing my daughters' handwriting change through the years: Melissa's backward "s" at age five and Kristin's large print, to match her outgoing personality. Kristin and Gary use a lot of space while Melissa and I write smaller. The randomness of the messages in content, shape, penmanship, and placement keeps me interested and feeling renewed every time I scan my humble work of art.

After the dinner plates are cleared away from the table on Christmas night, I lay several pencils in the center of the table, along with homemade biscotti, butter cookies, pies, and chocolates. While relaxing with our coffee and dessert, each family member reflects on the year and recalls an event, milestone, or something significant that happened to them during those past twelve months. Then we write our messages on the tablecloth—anywhere we want. Sometimes we write a message of inspiration or a wish for the coming year. I treasure the simple prayer "God Bless All My Family," written by my father in 1999.

After the holiday hubbub fades, the gifts are put away, and the needles from the Christmas tree are swept up, I sit down with my tablecloth of memories to begin embroidering. Sometimes I start right at the dining room table. Other times I nestle in a quiet corner chair in my living room with my sewing kit and start by separating the embroidery floss. I work slowly, striving to make each message legible with every stitch. My goal is to complete the embroidery by New Year's Eve. When the final stitch is made, I launder the tablecloth on the gentle cycle, then dry, fold, and store it until the following December.

This December will be the seventeenth time I spread my Christmas tablecloth on our dining room table. Sure, there are a couple of faded tea stains, but I simply cover them with a dinner plate or wine glass. Each year, more red and green appear and the white space diminishes. No worry. There's plenty of room for many years of memories to be recorded. What started out as a blank white canvas has been transformed into a cherished family heirloom.

Originally published in Chicken Soup for the Soul: It's Christmas, *October 2013.*

Say My Name

When my mother was pregnant with me, there was a teenager named Joyce living next door. Mom liked the name (and presumably, the girl), so she named me Joyce.

My brother had trouble pronouncing the "J" sound when he was a toddler, and what came out was "Goy-kee," after hearing his baby sister referred to as "Joycie." In our adult years, that moniker would occasionally be used in lighter moments with my siblings.

I don't know too many women named Joyce. Girls I grew up with had popular names like Kathy, Debbie, Patty, Maureen, and Maryann. It was distinctive being the only one in the class named Joyce.

I like my one-syllable name. Always have. It's simple, clear, and no one has ever mispronounced it. Thanks, Mom and Dad.

Where I'm From

I am from playing Whisper Down the Lane, Mother May I? and Red Light/Green Light. I am from a twin home on a maple tree-lined lane with a babbling brook running behind it.

I am from the family whose son was different. I am from a neighborhood of families whose names end in a vowel and who rallied to help my brother develop and socialize with higher functioning people.

I am from the City of Brotherly Love, where Eagles soar, Flyers skate, Sixers swoosh, and Phillies swing.

I am from Angelo's ice cream truck and Creamsicles at the skating rink.

I am from the Hotpoint refrigerator that was replaced by harvest gold kitchen appliances. I am from Pine Sol and lemon Pledge and the daily push of a Hoover upright.

I am from the cherry cabinet record player blaring Herb Alpert and John Philip Sousa on Saturday mornings and Peggy Lee at Christmastime.

I am from Saturday chores that stopped at noon for lunchmeat sandwiches on fresh Italian rolls. I am from Tastykakes, water ice in a paper cone, and soft pretzels.

I am from a pot of gravy on the stove and one-o'clock Sunday dinners of macaroni followed by meatball sandwiches in the late afternoon.

I am from desserts of fruit cocktail, Jell-O, and Sara Lee served on a Formica table with a Lazy Susan.

I am from moving to a new house with dogwood trees and yew bushes that surrounded the front porch with a squeaky glider.

I am from the plastic fruit in a bowl on the dining room table, the umbrella stand in the hallway, and the American eagle doorknocker. I am from the telephone cord that touched the floor.

I am from the bang of the basketball backboard in the driveway and the cluttered garage.

I am from lazy summer days at the pool, penny candy, a bicycle built for two, table hockey, World Book Encyclopedia, my mother's thirty-five-cent pack of Kent cigarettes, and my father's rusty handsaw.

I am from sharing the master bedroom with my two sisters. I am from braces on my teeth, pixie haircuts, and a cheerleading uniform.

I am from too many Catechism classes at the Catholic parish where my Italian last name was repeatedly mispronounced.

I am from holidays with lots of cousins and tender aunts named Nee Nee and Tootsie.

I am from Grandmom's homemade ravioli and pizzelles. I am from Grandpop who drank beer with Santa Claus every Christmas Eve and called us on the phone so we could to talk to the jolly man.

I am from the mother who told me to "be productive" every day and the father who said to "get along" with others.

I am from Sunday drives to the airport, dinners at Court Diner, and vacations down the shore.

I am from commuting to college, being the only woman

in the conference room, marrying an Irish New Englander, mothering two daughters, surviving Lyme disease, and starting a new career.

My Father, the Veteran

My father served in the 24th Infantry Division, 3rd Combat Engineers, building bridges in the Philippines during World War II. He was stationed in Leyte, where he spent a week in the hospital after contracting malaria.

Dad was on a ship to Okinawa when Truman dropped the bomb. Over the years, Dad frequently credited the president for saving his life.

In Japan, Dad was a staff sergeant who typed the morning report for the A, B, & C companies. He liked his mail clerk job and its perk of driving a Jeep. The captain trusted my father, whom he called "Poge." Dad chauffeured the captain and complied when asked to pick up a certain nurse at eleven p.m. and drive her to the captain's tent. Then Dad would return at four a.m. to bring the young woman back to her barracks.

Dad's service was about to end when the captain urged him to re-enlist for another five years. The captain said he'd promote Dad to battalion sergeant. So Dad wrote home to ask for his mother's advice.

A couple of weeks later, Dad was notified that he had a call from the States. He waited in the day room before being ushered to a phone. When he picked up the receiver, he heard his mother cry, "Don't you sign anything! Come home!"

Dad let his mother finish ranting and said, "Mom, why did you waste money making this overseas call? You could have opened the window and yelled and I'd have heard you."

Glad you made it home, Dad!

Battle Weary

Uncle Freddie served in the army during World War II. He was stationed in Central Europe. When the Battle of the Bulge broke out, General Patton ordered a forced march. My uncle's infantry division ran for twenty miles, full pack.

When they arrived at their destination, Uncle Freddie collapsed with fatigue. That night, the Germans bombed like crazy, killing many Americans. The next morning, the dead bodies were collected and put on a truck. When they reached for my uncle, he woke up. He had slept through the whole blitzkrieg.

Mom's Quotes

The more you do, the more you can do.

That was one of my mother's famous lines. She didn't like seeing her kids sitting around the house watching TV or telling her we were tired. Sometimes she'd follow with the opposite and say: *The more you lay around, the lazier you become.*

In keeping with her no-nonsense, action-oriented days, she said: *Let's get done! Be productive. Be productive every day.*

If my siblings or I woke up not feeling well, hoping to avoid school, she said: *Walk to school. You'll feel better.*

When my sisters or I came downstairs in a new outfit, she said: *Adorable.*

If I expressed disappointment or lack of achievement, she said: *You should have . . .*

If there was a family debate about a world fact, she said: *Go get the encyclopedia.*

If my siblings or I disagreed with her decision, she said: *I'm the mother!*

If we lost a personal item and insisted we couldn't find it, she said: *Look harder!*

If we moped around for no good reason, she answered: *Get happy!*

If I debated whether or not to buy something a tad expensive, she said: *Buy it if you like it!*

Whenever Mom imparted unsolicited words of wisdom to me, particularly as a new homeowner and new mother, she said: *My mother never told me . . . I wish my mother had told me . . .*

If I was on the fence about what to do, she said: *Do whatever makes you happy.*

After hanging up from a long call, the phone would ring a minute later and I'd answer to hear her say: *One more thing . . .*

And finally, *You'll miss me when I'm gone.*

Blood Sisters

The bubble of blood sat on her fingertip like a tiny holly berry. She had already pricked herself with a safety pin, but I was having trouble jabbing the point into the flesh of my index finger.

Gina and I were first cousins the same age but we wanted to be closer. We negotiated sleepovers as often as possible even though we lived a half mile apart and went to the same elementary school.

"Try another finger," she said as we stood in our nightgowns at the open windowsill of her bedroom that summer morning.

"My pinkie?"

"Any one. C'mon, Joyce, I'm waiting," she said, giggling nervously.

"I'm scared," I told her.

"Don't be scared. If I can do it, you can." Her laugh relaxed me. I closed my eyes and pierced the fleshy underside of my ring finger.

"You did it! Quick!"

We pressed fingertip to fingertip and watched our combined blood run and rub together. With the ceremony complete, we grinned at each other in triumph. Then we separated our hands, leaving crimson smudges as the only proof of our ritual.

"Now we are blood sisters," Gina said. "That's even closer than cousins."

"Yeah," I said. "It'll be our secret forever."

Just then, we heard my aunt call us for breakfast.

"We better wash our hands before my mother comes up," Gina said.

Shoulder to shoulder, my new blood sister and I tiptoed barefooted into the bathroom, upturned fingertips leading the way. We giggled while rinsing our hands together under the faucet and watched swirls of red water circle down the drain.

Easter Sunday

Easter meant I got to carry a purse and wear white gloves and a new straw hat. In a classic 1965 family photo, I clasped my hands, feeling stylish in the herringbone coat with black velvet buttons and piping on the collar.

My big sister wore a straw hat too, while my little sister donned a navy tam. My brother looked spiffy in a jacket and tie. Mom always made sure we looked presentable wherever we went. She did a lot on a tight budget.

Before going to church, we'd have our family Easter egg hunt. I can still hear my father saying, "Warm, warmer, hot! HOT!" while we searched all the usual places for our colored hard-boiled eggs: under pillow cushions, inside plants, on the windowsill, behind the encyclopedias.

For days, we'd eat slices of coconut cream chocolate eggs while the pastel versions lay in a bowl untouched until Mom made egg salad sandwiches.

One year, my grandparents came over with a large cardboard box. Ten little chickadees—nine yellow and one black. Who knows what they were thinking bringing these creatures into our house? We just stared down at the web-footed babies skittering around. I don't think they lasted a week before Mom carried the box to the car, drove to a nearby creek, and turned the box on its side. We never were pet people.

Family Doctor Makes Final House Call

Do you remember when family doctors made house calls?

My mother chose a neighborhood family practice of three physicians to care for my siblings and me. The elder doctor was gruff. A second, handsome one made women swoon. And the third was young.

One afternoon, Mom called young Dr. Braunfeld and asked if he would stop by the house after office hours. She wanted him to examine Jimmy, my preteen brother, who kept coughing and insisting that something was stuck in his throat.

That evening, the doctor came to the house and discovered Jimmy had a piece of a toothpick lodged in the back of his mouth. Dr. Braunfeld used a medical instrument to extract the bit and relieved Jimmy of his discomfort.

Mom noticed Dr. Braunfeld sweating after his deft handwork. She invited him into the kitchen to relax. He drank a glass of milk and ate an Oreo. Then he confessed to my parents that the procedure he'd just completed was the first time he'd used his medical training outside of a routine flu or earache.

Forty-five years later, a friend from the old neighborhood had an appointment with the same Dr. Braunfeld. When my family's name came up, the doctor asked for my father's phone number. The next night, he called Dad (who had moved out of state long ago) and they spent twenty minutes chatting.

Decades after the toothpick incident, Dr. Braunfeld took time to pay respect to my father. It was another memorable house call made by our "young" family doctor.

A Moment with My Mother

As one of four children, it was rare to get a moment alone with my mother.

"C'mon Joyce, let's take a picture together, just you and me," she said, taking my hand.

We were in Puerto Rico on a Christmas family vacation in 1974—a big splurge for my parents. It was the first time any of us kids had been on a plane and something extraordinary for a family who lived modestly.

One night on our way to dinner, I trailed the others walking through the outdoor café of the hotel when Mom suggested taking the photo. She must have sensed something was bothering me. I'd felt self-conscious about my teenage body and was constantly worried about getting fat. That afternoon on the beach, I'd eaten a cheeseburger and fries and drank virgin piña coladas that left me feeling bloated.

I tugged down the gauze midriff top Mom had bought for me (I'd wanted the long, flowing one). I certainly didn't want to have my photo taken.

"Mom, do we have to?"

The teenager in me resisted the silliness of posing with my mother in public before finally acquiescing. I had no choice. She put her arm around me and wouldn't let go.

At age forty-three, Mom wore a V-neck, sleeveless batik

dress that showed off her shapely legs. She exuded confidence and glowed with happiness. She was so relaxed in that tropical oasis, far from the routine of cooking meals and doing laundry at home.

"Babe," she called to my father, who walked a few steps ahead carrying the Kodak Instamatic camera. "Quick, take one of Joyce and me."

Several months after Mom died, my sister found the photo. It wasn't until I looked at it that I realized it is the only photo I have of just Mom and me.

My mother was wise in many ways. She read people well. That afternoon, decades ago, Mom intuited that I needed some attention. I'm grateful she stopped to provide me comfort and insisted on capturing that fleeting moment.

Grandmom's Chair

I rarely saw my grandmother sit down. When arriving at her row home in West Philadelphia, she'd be in the kitchen hunched over the Formica table, kneading dough for ravioli as the skin on her upper arms jiggled.

Even after my family was seated for dinner, she'd stand at the head of the dining table, still in her apron, and proudly serve us an authentic Italian meal. Steam rose from the bowl of meatballs and sausage. The house smelled like an Italian restaurant.

After we finished eating, she'd stand at the ceramic sink to wash all the plates, pots, and pans. She'd reach for the dish towel slung over her shoulder and slowly tread in her sturdy shoes to the dining room, living room, and porch to pick up stray glasses and napkins. Occasionally, she'd amble to the sideboard, open a drawer, and give my siblings and me a deck of cards or a quarter to go buy penny candy at the corner store.

All the while, Grandmom's Queen Anne side chair remained empty.

Somehow that chair made it to our house after Grandmom died, and then Mom gave it to me when I moved into my first apartment. The antique with faded red and beige fabric wasn't exactly an item a young twenty-something would select, but when you're starting with nothing, any piece of furniture will do.

In 2011, I took Grandmom's chair to be reupholstered and was surprised when the craftsman showed me the horsehair and hog's-hair stuffing. Then he turned the chair over and pointed to the unmarred tag glued under the seat. It's unclear when Grandmom had bought the chair, but she had had it reupholstered in 1964.

My upholsterer cut around the tag so I could have it framed. Now it hangs on the wall above the chair.

I love this bit of family history and feel lucky to own Grandmom's chair.

At the Dinner Table

"The family meal is the nursery of democracy. I really do think we literally civilize our children at the table. That's where they learn to take turns and to share and to argue."

— Michael Pollan

When my daughters were young, I read something similar to this quote in a parenting book. The simple act resonated with me, so I vowed to set the table and cook a nutritional dinner at least five times a week. (Fridays were reserved for pizza and on Saturday nights we usually went out to a family restaurant.) Sure, there were times when I had to work late or the children had soccer practice, but we made up for it at lunch or breakfast together.

The family meal is also the place where children learn manners. Saying grace first, using a napkin and utensils properly, asking to be excused, and bringing one's plate to the sink are important lessons. Manners matter.

When Kristin was about six years old, she was seated at the dinner table animatedly telling a story. Her younger sister, Melissa, the quiet one, was eager to say something and tried to find a break in Kristin's epic tale. When Kristin told Melissa to wait because she wasn't finished, Melissa stretched her arm across the table, leaned her head down, and cried, "Kristin, you talk too much!"

I had to suppress laughter because I saw how genuine and frustrated my little one was.

"Okay, Melissa. Your turn," I said, rubbing her back.

Still draped across the table, she burst into tears and said, "I forgot what I wanted to say!"

Over the years, I've loved hearing my daughters' stories about school, friends, day camp, jobs, goals, and more. Our dinner table has been a valuable source of learning for me, too.

A Giraffe

My young daughter came in from the cold one winter day and asked me to help her remove her snow boots. I knelt down on the floor and told her to wait a second as I reached over to close the interior door and said, "There's a draft coming in."

My rosy-cheeked darling turned her head toward the door with a curious look on her face and said, "I don't see a giraffe."

There, There

My twenty-one-year-old sleeps on the couch next to me while I write on the porch this breezy summer day. Last night, she tiptoed into my bedroom at one a.m. and said, "Mom, I don't feel well."

I rose from the bed and went through the predictable parental diagnostics: "What's wrong?" I asked, automatically putting my hand on her forehead and ruling out a fever. She moaned.

"What hurts?" I asked.

"My stomach."

"An ache? A throb? What?"

"Shooting pain."

"Show me." We ruled out appendicitis when she circled her hand around her tanned, flat belly. She hadn't gone out with friends after dinner, so I assumed something she ate had disagreed with her.

"What did you eat after dinner?" I asked.

"Nothing."

"Did you go to the bathroom?"

"Yes."

"Did you overexert yourself at the gym?"

"No."

She climbed into my bed and Mr. MOTM (my husband, Mr.

Musing Off the Mat) shuffled to the guest room. Still restless after a few minutes, she moved to the bedroom chair and asked for a heating pad. Then she dragged herself back and forth to the bathroom a couple of times. On the third visit, I followed and held her hair away from her face as she retched.

"There, there," I said, pulling the words out of thin air. I remember reading somewhere that repeating "there, there," creates a comforting effect—something to do with the phonetics of the word. When I became a mother, I thought it sounded like an old lady refrain. Yet, a maternal instinct kicked in and the refrain emerged from my lips.

I stayed with my daughter as she washed up and then asked her if she wanted to sleep in my bed. "Yeah," she answered weakly. After I placed a pillow under her knees, she fell asleep within minutes.

I lay awake thinking of the wee morning hours twenty-one years ago when, as an infant, she'd lie next to me after being nursed. I'd stare at her eyelashes and watch her belly rise and fall with each tiny breath. Last night and this afternoon, I watched again as my first-born, a grown woman now, respired in peaceful slumber.

There, there.

Happy Birthday, Dear Brother

Happy 60th Birthday to my brother, Jimmy, who inspires me every day.

Jimmy, who has overcome intellectual and physical challenges his entire life. Who uses his abilities and doesn't think about his disabilities. Who demonstrates achievement over adversity.

Jimmy, who dutifully spent his childhood going from doctor to doctor without complaint.

Jimmy, who endured teen years of prejudice and bullying without resentment or retribution.

Jimmy, who coped in his lonely twenties by developing skills and job training when his neighborhood pals went to college and married.

Jimmy, who spent his thirties with our parents while my two sisters and I left home, married, and began families of our own.

Jimmy, who, in his forties, complied with my aging parents' agonizing decision to relocate him to live semi-independently in a supervised apartment.

Jimmy, who, in his fifties, retired from part-time work at the supermarket and entered an adult day program, where he now thrives.

Jimmy, who taught himself how to use a computer tablet, reads several newspapers every day, quotes sports statistics, discusses current events, keeps his room neat and organized, is always on time, completes jigsaw puzzles with ease, and has a powerful golf swing.

Jimmy, who calls his sisters at seven a.m. to announce the weather or latest headline and asks what we're doing for the next holiday.

Jimmy, who has an excellent memory, a healthy appetite, an infectious laugh, and unconditional love for his family.

Happy Birthday, Jimmy. You are my touchstone.

My Life in 100 Words

I'm a middle child and not even squarely in the middle. As the third of four children, I wanted a definitive label like my siblings. In our Dodge Dart, my baby sister won the coveted seat up front, between our Mom and Dad. I had no choice but to be sandwiched between my older sister and brother, who had window seats. My feet straddled the hump.

Fifty years later, my unabashed, honest brother reminded me of the pecking order. He phoned and said, "I called Lynne. She's not home. Then I called Alison. She didn't answer. So I called you."

My Date with Dad

Dad wore a suit jacket for his date with me to the opening film of the Lighthouse International Film Festival on Long Beach Island.

Off we went to an unpretentious venue, walking on twenty feet of red carpet (without paparazzi) before entering the small auditorium. We sat near an exit, just in case Dad didn't feel well.

The movie about a broken family started off slowly. We glanced at each other with skeptical eyes. I figured the film would get better. It didn't. I knew Dad wanted to leave, but he wouldn't want to call attention to himself.

I leaned in and whispered, "Dad, we can leave whenever you want." He's eighty-six. I can't afford to waste his time.

"I'm okay," he said.

We suffered through another thirty minutes and saw a few people leave before I nudged him and said, "Let's go."

As we walked arm in arm across the gravel parking lot in spitting rain, Dad let out a big sigh and said, "Boy, was that a stinker."

"That's for sure."

"Who's the DIE-rector of that movie? Is he here?"

I paged through the program and told Dad the director's name. When Dad repeated the name, mispronouncing it, I lost it. The whole scene struck me as hilarious.

"I'd like to tell that DIE-rector what I thought of his lousy movie."

Each time Dad said "DIE-rector," I laughed more.

"Waste of my time. And you said that's the featured film? Dumb DIE-rector," he said shaking his head side to side.

We climbed into my SUV and Dad was still phew-ing and geez-ing. With each of his zingers, my chuckles turned to giggles turned to belly laughs turned to a full-throttle-whooping-can't-catch-my-breath-howling until tears rolled down my cheeks. I hadn't laughed that hard in years.

He simply responded to my unbridled spring with a soft laugh.

As my cachinnation slowed to a titter, I managed to ask, "Dad, what do you say we go for an ice cream cone?"

"Yeah, that sounds good."

A few miles down the empty road, we sauntered into an ice cream parlor as its only customers. He asked for vanilla fudge and I ordered chocolate chip—double scoop for both. We brought our cones back to the car and I started the ignition, thinking he was eager to get home.

"Where're you going? Let's eat here," Dad said, holding his cone with admiration.

Yeah, I thought, what was I rushing for? We still had our date to finish.

While we ate our ice cream in the car, I called my older sister Lynne to relate the story of ditching the movie made by a certain DIE-rector. I could barely get the words out because I laughed and cried all over again. Dad never missed a beat, slurping contentedly, with a half smile.

In the past four-and-a-half years since my mother died, Dad and I have probably had more one-on-one time together than in all the time I grew up. He's given me more gifts of time and wisdom than I can recite. The strong work ethic he modeled and the loyalty to his wife and family are among his greatest gifts.

We've laughed and cried through happy and difficult milestones. He taught me to ride a bike, to dive, and to drive. Together, we dealt with allergies and hay fever. He took me to look at colleges, helped set up my first apartment, and drove seven hours in a snowstorm with Mom to be at my house for Christmas. He cradled my baby daughters with love that brought tears to my eyes. He's always been there for me.

On my recent date with Dad, sitting in a parking lot at sunset in early June, he made me laugh with abandon. That laughter came from the tips of my toes and evolved into a full-body release that I didn't know I needed. The grief over losing Mom and worries about Dad living alone that I'd carried with me for so long melted away in that moment of freedom.

Indeed, my father gave me a night to remember.

A Winter Visit with Dad

One February morning, I gladly left the snow banks of New England to visit Dad in New Jersey. The further south I drove that cold, sunny day, the more my mood lifted.

Visits with Dad consist of familiar routine, no matter what the season: grocery shopping, cooking, bill paying, auditing his checkbook, laundry, light housekeeping, and, best of all, reminiscing. He tells the same stories about the war, his parents, his youth, and, of course, Mom. It doesn't matter to me that I've heard them before, because I love the sound of his voice.

Around six a.m., the front door groans open and I know Dad is eager to retrieve the *Philadelphia Inquirer*. I lie in bed a little while longer. By the time I greet him at the kitchen table with a morning kiss, he summarizes the news for me.

"It's fifteen degrees outside. No snow in the forecast."

"Oh, that's good," I say, opening the blinds. "Look, it's sunny out."

"Nobody died," he reports.

Phew. He's lost a few friends in recent months.

"I have one problem."

"What's that, Dad?"

"I can't get the last word in the Jumble," he says, sliding the folded paper toward me.

"Let's see." A couple minutes later, I say, "Burlap. It's never an everyday word."

On our first day together, we always head to Shop Rite early. He pushes the cart with a measured pace while I fill it with the standard fare: bananas, Cheerios, provolone, meat for Italian dinners, vegetables, and chicken for soup.

I pick up another set of sixteen-ounce Ziploc containers so I can fill his freezer with single-serving meals. If you have an elderly parent, I recommend buying these. They're easy to use and your parent doesn't have to fuss with portioning from an oversized Tupperware bowl.

"Let's stop at Kohl's," Dad says, sliding into the passenger seat. "I need socks."

"Sure, Dad."

We find the socks with minimal elastic and I buy a pair of slippers to keep at his house.

"Where to next?" I ask on our way out of the store, strolling arm in arm. I want to go to the soft pretzel store and I know he does too, so I wait for his cue.

He turns his head and gives me a knowing smile. We break into laughter. Well, the shop is on the way home anyway. Ooh, and today is buy three get three free. For only two dollars. Who cares about the calories? We mm-mm while chomping on the warm, salty dough even before I turn on the ignition.

Back home, the cooktop is crowded with pots of simmering, savory goodness: beef stew, chicken soup, lentil soup, and meatballs and sausage in gravy. Later, I fill individual glass custard cups with Jell-O. While I'm busy in the kitchen, he sits at the table and fills his weekly pill dispenser.

I love to dote on Dad. It makes me feel useful. I have a purpose.

After dinner, we settle in for a cozy night with a cup of tea. He watches Fox TV under an afghan and rests his feet on the ottoman. I sit nearby in my pajamas and robe with a crossword puzzle.

"I feel guilty," Dad says, after muting the TV.

"Why?" I ask, lowering my eyeglasses.

"Because," he says turning to me. "You should be with your family."

"I am with my family."

My Father's Hands

My father's hands are soft now. Like the finest, buttery leather. They're thinner, no longer with a ring. The two of us hold hands while saying grace.

There once was a time when our family of six sat at the dinner table together. Dad broke the Italian bread and lifted a glass of Chianti. That came after a day of lifting steel rods and carrying lumber while building bridges and skyscrapers in the sweltering heat and numbing cold of Philadelphia. He'd come home from work and unlace his dirt-dusted boots in the kitchen. Then he'd go into the powder room to wash his hands with Lava soap and rub in Corn Huskers lotion before heading upstairs to shower before dinner.

My father's firm, strong hands never stopped working. At home, they wielded a hammer to build a deck out back. They hung paneling and laid floor tile in the basement. They washed cars, scrubbed windows, inflated bike tires, trimmed hedges, pushed the mower, unclogged toilets, and replaced countless lightbulbs.

Those same hands gingerly rolled meatballs and kneaded dough to make gnocchi. "This is the way my mother did it," he said proudly, one hand mixing the flour and egg on the table and the other hand behind his back at waist level, palm out.

My father's hands reassured me when I was afraid to

dive into the pool. He stood in the five-foot level while I wrapped my toes around the concrete lip of the pool, shivering, my knees knocking. "You can do it!" he said, those big paddles covering the tops of my feet. And when I finally dove into the water and came up for air, he grinned, splashed the water, clapped his wet hands, and said, "Atta girl!"

My father's hands covered mine on top of the stick shift of our blue VW bug when it was perched at the top of a hill and I feared we'd roll backward. "You can do it!" he said again with a reassuring tap.

When I had mono and my fever wouldn't break, my father's hands massaged rubbing alcohol on the backs of my legs. "You'll get better soon," he said.

My father's hands packed the Toyota Corolla when I left home. They hammered nails into the walls of my first apartment and assembled my bed. They hoisted an oversized couch onto the second story porch and through the sliding doors. "Be careful," he said tenderly, leaving me on my own.

My father gave my hand in marriage to my waiting bridegroom. "Take good care of her," he'd said. A few years later, he cradled his granddaughters and pushed their carriages with his head held high and a huge smile on his face.

My father wrapped his arms around me and comforted me with gentle strokes on my back when Mom died. "I miss her, too," he said, his voice cracking.

These days, my father's hands grab the railing when leaving and entering the house. His palms graze chairs and the countertop when moving cautiously from room to room. His fingers flutter a bit when starting the zipper on his jacket, but he still signs his name with graceful care.

We walk hand in hand now, down to the bay. He holds tightly and leans closer to me, arm to arm.

No matter the wind or cold, my father's hands warm me.

My Most Memorable Christmas Gift

My most memorable Christmas gift was delivered weeks before the holiday. It wasn't wrapped in red and green paper with a bow. It wasn't purchased at a favorite store nor was it something I asked for.

My parents had driven seven hours from Pennsylvania to Massachusetts for an early celebration with my husband, baby daughter, and me.

After leaving their luggage in the hallway, my father went back to the car. Mom clasped her hands and brimmed with excitement as Dad carried a big cooler into the house. He beamed when placing it on the kitchen floor.

"Instead of giving you a pretty sweater, this year Daddy and I decided to give you home-cooked meals for Christmas," Mom said. "We know how hard you work and how busy you are. This will make your life easier."

I stood in the kitchen with my baby on my hip and watched in awe as Mom identified the mouthwatering, prepackaged meals she lifted from the cooler.

Lemon chicken, string beans almondine, meat loaf, sweet potatoes, beef stew, meatballs, sausage and gravy—all labeled in Ziploc bags and containers.

"I can't believe you two did this," I said. "It must have taken days."

"All you have to do is heat them up," Mom said, filling the freezer.

"This is the best!" I said, hugging my parents.

Mom and Dad have selected beautiful presents through the years—jewelry that I still wear and decorative pieces displayed throughout my home. However, that bounty of love was by far the most memorable gift they ever gave me. In doing so, they nourished my family and nourished my soul.

A World of Thanks

When my daughter returned from her semester abroad, I hugged her and didn't want to let go. I had worried about her safety the entire time she was gone despite weekly FaceTime calls and updates via text messages.

I had tucked a letter in her luggage, encouraging her to experience as much culture as possible. She did just that, promising to travel in a group and to be cautious while visiting eight countries and countless points of interest.

So, on Christmas Eve, when she presented her father and me with a homemade gift, I got choked up again just as I did when she had left four months earlier. She had framed a collage of photos of herself holding signs around famous European landmarks in Ireland, Venice, Munich, London, Paris, Amsterdam, and Barcelona. In each location, she held a sign with a single word on it. The collage of seven photos spelled out this sentence:

Thank you for giving me the world.

Morning

My footsteps on the wooden boards of the easement create a baritone clunk as the roar of the surf and salty air beckon me. Through grassy dunes and the irregular slant of fencing, I walk until the sea comes into view. My heartbeat slows. There's no better way to restore myself than to go to the beach on Long Beach Island with a cup of coffee before the crowds arrive.

I sit on the dark green bench and place the cup next to me. Stretching my arms across the back of the bench, I tilt my head skyward, close my eyes, and offer my heart. My mother's voice whispers, "Breathe in the salt air. It's good for you." The wind lifts my hair and cools my scalp.

Bending to take off my socks and shoes, I bury my feet in the sand, wiggle my toes, and massage the top of each foot with the sole of the other. Mom used to say walking on the beach was the best way to exfoliate the skin because the sand acted as natural pumice. I dig the outer edges of my hands into the gritty cleanser, lift my palms with a small mound, and then rub them together as I would under a faucet. Granules float in the breeze.

The pristine sand closest to me is dimpled with the miniature dew marks of morning. Its texture changes halfway to the ocean's edge, where tire tracks from the beach patrol truck bisect the beach. The sand near the surf line is flat at low tide where little waves wash away footprints of an early morning jogger.

As I sip coffee, the hot liquid coats my throat. Its aroma wakens me with the anticipation of a new day. Like Mom, I do my best thinking in the morning, our favorite part of the day. The loud, constant hum of the surf calms me. The ocean is charcoal gray and its breakwater looks like white feather boas dancing ashore. A black sock and small piece of driftwood lie lonely, like scabs on the earth's skin.

Gulls soar against the faded blue sky and stratus clouds. The honking birds float down to the beach, peck, peck, pecking, searching for their breakfast. The sun shines so brightly from behind the clouds that I cannot look straight up. I make a visor, hands to brow, and squint at the sun, glistening like a silver sheet on the surface of the sea.

To my left, two Adirondack chairs face each other. I wonder about who nestled there the night before and what intimate words might have been spoken. Were they lovers or were they mother and daughter like Mom and me?

The beach was one of the few places where I saw Mom completely relax. Sometimes she would fly a kite, then tie it to the wooden arm of her sand chair and get a big kick out of the rainbow of silk fluttering against July skies. She'd collect sea glass before it became fashionable, holding her palm out when returning from a walk to show her newly found treasures. Intellectually curious, she would open a box of Trivial Pursuit cards to entertain and challenge us on those carefree summer days. Her smile was wider and easier then.

My coffee cup is drained and it is time to leave this peaceful oasis. Gazing slowly at the horizon from left to right, the curve of the earth presents itself, reminding me that my worries are small. I walk two more blocks north, sinking my bare feet into the earth at its softest. Cutting through the fenced dune path, I glance back to see Mom once more in the glory of the morning.

The Kiss

In her late thirties, my mother bought a twelve-inch-high replica of *The Kiss*, by Auguste Rodin. She displayed the sculpture of two naked lovers on top of Dad's dresser.

As a preteen, I considered the art scandalous. I curiously examined the muscular man and curvy woman sitting in a romantic embrace whenever I put away Dad's clean socks and T-shirts. It mystified me why Mom selected this piece of art, unlike anything else in our modest home containing prints, antiques, and plants.

When Dad came home after a hard day on a construction site where he labored as an ironworker foreman, he'd take a shower and then nap on his bed before coming downstairs for dinner with the family.

Occasionally, I heard him shout, "Rosemarie! I need help picking out my socks."

"I can do it, Daddy!" I said the first time hearing his plea, eager to help him separate navy from black.

"Here, this one's black," I offered.

"No," he said, tossing the pair back into the drawer rather cheerfully. "Get your mother. She's the only one who can pick out my socks."

I left the room dejected and relayed the message to Mom in the kitchen. She walked up the stairs, swinging her hips and letting out a giggle. Then I heard the bedroom door close.

Recently, I helped Dad purge old shirts from his closet. I glanced at his dresser—the same one bought in 1952 when my parents married—and noticed the unique piece was gone.

"Dad, what happened to *The Kiss* sculpture Mom bought you? Did you move it from the top of your dresser?"

"We lost it when we moved to this house," he said wistfully. "Your mother and I looked everywhere. Never found it."

"That's a shame," I said, gathering up a pile of threadbare shirts. "Are we all done here, Dad?"

"Just a minute." He padded across the room, kissed his fingertips, tapped them on the shiny wooden box atop his dresser, and said, "See you later, honey."

When God Winked

Dad and I went to the eye doctor. While sitting in the bright, large waiting room of the converted mill building, we were trying to figure out how the N. C. Wyeth print, *The Giant*, got lost. Mom had bought it more than twenty-five years ago and hung it over the couch in their old house.

"Did you check the attic?" Dad asked.

"Yes. I searched everywhere," I answered. "Do you think Mom gave it to someone?"

"I don't think so. She loved that picture."

We figured it must have gotten lost in the move to the house where they'd retired, perhaps while their furnishings were in storage for two months.

A minute later, the vision technician ushered us to a smaller waiting room.

"I'm going to ask Alison," I said, sitting across from Dad. "Maybe she knows what happened to it."

I pulled out my phone and began texting my sister, when I heard Dad say, "There it is."

I looked up from the phone to see Dad gazing above my head. My first instinct was that Dad's vision is worse than I thought—maybe he's seeing what he wants to see. Or, God forbid, maybe he's losing his mind.

I turned around and nearly fell out of the chair. There it

was, indeed. Hanging on the wall of the smaller waiting room, directly above my head, was the exact print—N. C. Wyeth's famous work, framed with a light shining on it.

Dad and I locked eyes in awe.

"It's Mom," I said. "She's here with us."

When Your Child Graduates College

You start planning for her college education when she's in utero. You open a separate bank account. You buy educational toys and lots of books. You go to all the parent-teacher conferences and review the high school curriculum. You prep her for SATs and make college visits. Then, the summer before she leaves, you fill the house with more stuff than you can imagine will fit into a tiny dorm room.

You stand in the center of her bedroom and stare. She hasn't left much behind—a photo album, her high school graduation cap, a piggy bank. Weren't you just reading her a bedtime story? Didn't you just give her medicine for an earache?

She settles in and you get happy calls. Then you get a few frantic calls. She's panicked about an exam or doesn't like a certain professor. She's sick. She's tired. She's probably hung over. Boyfriend problems. She's happy again. She's low on cash. You add money to her bank account and remind her to be more responsible with her spending. You send care packages. A Hallmark card. A Dunkin' Donuts gift card.

The first time she comes home, you buy flowers, prepare her favorite meals, and do her laundry. When she returns to campus, you settle into your new routine. It's nice not hearing the long showers or the foot traffic up and down the stairs. The backpack and flip-flops aren't blocking the kitchen desk.

Dinner is easier minus one. You sleep better not watching the clock, waiting for the front door to open late at night.

During the next three years, you are happy to see her when she comes home, but you don't rush out of the house to greet her like you did the first year. She flies in and out. She does her own laundry. You kiss her goodbye again. You're relieved when she returns to school and your home is restored to the quiet you relish and the quiet that sometimes aches.

She gets a job on campus. She has a nice circle of friends. She's made good choices.

You make the final tuition payment and it feels like a virtual pay raise the following month.

Graduation day arrives. There's a lump in your throat as you listen to "Pomp and Circumstance." Flashbacks to her as a baby and toddler. Pride. Joy. Smiles. Photos. A sigh of relief.

A new chapter begins.

Shopping with My Sister

My younger sister, Alison, defines a successful shopping spree as a "three bagger," that is, carrying at least three bags to the car. Ambling through the mall last weekend, looking for nothing in particular, she said with a concerned tone, "I don't know . . . we're thirty minutes in, and still no bags."

Sometimes I have difficulty with small decisions while shopping. I once held up a dress and asked Alison if she liked it. I must have been feeling down because she responded, "If you want to be laid out in it," without breaking her stride, her eyebrows raised and head cocked to the side with that "Are you crazy?" visage.

I've been in a dressing room and will open the door for her opinion. "Take it off," she'll say flatly. I love her bluntness and don't bother debating a fashion mishap.

On the other hand, she's encouraging and quick to say, "Buy it" when I'm about to return a dress to the rack, thinking I don't need it.

Unlike me, Alison wears clothes that are short, sparkly, and sexy and pulls it off on her five-foot-nine-inch frame. On this trip, she pointed out a zip-up hoodie at Lululemon for me to try on, insisting I should go a size smaller. I opted to buy a yoga top. Bag one.

One time, we were shopping in one of those boutiques

without restrooms. Alison stood at the counter squeezing her thighs and politely asked to use the employee restroom. When the sales associate answered no, my sister said, "Either you're going to let me use your bathroom or you're going to be mopping up a puddle right here in front of your checkout counter." The young sales associate relented.

While admiring handbags in Lord & Taylor, I showed her a cross-body style. "The clasp looks like a tongue. You want that on your hip?" she replied and kept browsing. She found one that met her specs: zip-top closure and flat bottom. Bag two.

After our salad lunch, the hunt continued. We petted shoes in Nordstrom that neither of us needed and were too expensive.

Finally, we decided to hit TJMaxx. Bingo! In no time, we scored bags three, four, and five.

Always Something There to Remind Me

He flew from Boston and I from New York for a Florida vacation in the spring of 1985. I was excited about a romantic getaway with the guy I had started dating a few months earlier.

"What started out as friendship has grown stronger . . ."

I felt nervous because I had vowed not to date anyone at work. However, he was full of life, smart, unpretentious, and he made me laugh.

"I tell myself that I can't hold out forever . . ."

We soaked in the salt air and warm, ocean breezes. After our first day in the sun, the right side of my face and the left side of his face were burnt from looking at each other in conversation for hours on end. With our coloring lopsided, we switched sides the next day and continued talking and laughing as our books lay on the sand untouched.

"I'm getting closer than I ever thought I might . . ."

As we cruised over the Clearwater Causeway Bridge on the way to the airport, REO Speedwagon came on the radio.

"Can't Fight This Feeling Anymore" had topped the charts for weeks and we instantly looked at each other when we heard the song's familiar introductory notes.

We shouted those perfect song lyrics to each other. I couldn't stop smiling because seated next to me, crooning beautifully off key, was my future husband.

"It's time to bring this ship into the shore and throw away the oars forever."

The image of us cruising in a convertible over calm, blue waters under a cloudless sky with the sun shining down on us is one I'll never forget. That morning—that specific scene of song and love—ranks as the most carefree moment of my life.

Ushered Over with Grace

Aunt Dolores was the quintessential hostess. She welcomed my family into her well-appointed home on holidays and many other occasions.

As a young girl, I'd hurry into the kitchen, where Aunt Dolores greeted me with a big smile and a perfumed kiss. I admired the way she prepared appetizers, tended to a roast in the oven, and poured drinks in her stylish dress, jingling charm bracelet, and manicured nails. As an adult, I'd come to admire the deep faith she relied on to help her cope with life's challenges.

Aunt Dolores made guests feel special by serving holiday dinners using silver chafing dishes, fine china, and beautiful linens.

"That's carrot cake, dear," she said, placing dessert plates on the sideboard one Easter, when she saw me staring.

"A cake made with carrots?" the preteen in me asked.

"Yes! Try it. You'll love it, especially with that cream cheese frosting," she said, giving me a gentle nudge and a wink.

At Christmastime, my siblings, cousins, and I would sing and dance on the marble floor in the foyer to "Jingle Bells." Then we'd gather in the living room to continue caroling, sitting cross-legged on the Oriental rugs that lay below shelves displayed with a collection of Wedgwood.

In summer, Aunt Dolores would invite us to swim in the pool in her expansive back yard that was surrounded by apple and cherry trees we'd climb. That beautiful pool area was featured on the front page of the Home and Garden section of the *Philadelphia Inquirer* one Sunday, showing Aunt Dolores holding a red geranium.

A white, wrought iron, ice cream table and two matching red-and-white-striped chairs were situated on the indented side of the kidney-shaped pool. When Aunt Dolores decided to redecorate, she gave me the set to use in the kitchen of my first apartment.

During her last five-and-a-half years, my relationship with Aunt Dolores deepened. I'd call her on the phone, feeling a need to be close to her after the death of my mother (her sister) and then Aunt Dolores's husband. I wanted to hear her voice and recall the joy I felt as a kid in her home.

She'd first ask about my family. Then I'd prompt her to tell me stories about her youth and my grandparents, which she did, often in a melancholy voice. She'd get excited, though, when talking about her beloved Phillies and my alma mater's basketball team, readily citing player statistics. "And how about our Villanova Wildcats this year!" But her favorite topic was her four daughters, grandchildren, and great-grandchildren. When talking about them, superlatives were the norm: "Fabulous!" "Terrific!" "Wonderful!" She always ended our phone conversations with a prayer.

Aunt Dolores faithfully attended Catholic mass and prayed constantly. Near the end, she told me, "It's all in God's hands."

When the cancer returned and her health continued to decline, she kept a fighting spirit, even laughing during her last hours. "I've had a good life," she once told me. She stayed mentally strong until the very end.

That's when Aunt Dolores said she heard music and saw her mother and husband. With church hymns playing softly, she prayed while holding hands with her daughters and was ushered over with grace.

Snowstorm Phone Call

It's difficult for my eighty-eight-year-old father to grasp technology. Concerned about the snowstorm, he called my sister at her office, where she runs a small business.

"Where are you?" he asked worriedly.

"I'm at the office," Lynne answered.

"No, you're not. I just called there and the message on the answering machine said the office is closed."

"Dad, I'm sitting at my desk. You called me on my cell phone."

"Oh. Well, your office is closed."

I Am That Woman

I am that woman now—the one my younger, impatient self watched guide an elderly parent across the parking lot into the medical center ever so slowly.

After living my entire adult life 350 miles from my parents, now Dad lives five miles from me in an assisted living residence. He made the brave and wise decision to move on his own. Thankfully, my siblings and I were spared that decision. Dad knew he couldn't take another desolate winter alone in his island home. Seven years had passed since my mother died, and in that time Dad mourned the loss of too many friends.

The signs of readiness were there: a minor car accident, struggling to read fine print, poor eating habits, dehydration, sleeping too much, forgetting to take his meds. He'd taped a note to the back door: Check gas on stove. (I'd learn later that he'd left the stove on one morning. Fortunately, the housekeeper had arrived an hour after he'd driven off.) He missed his favorite diner that converted to a taco restaurant. The Kiwanis meeting schedule changed. He was confused and sad without routine.

Although it can never be home, when Dad arrived at his sunny new apartment, he noticed we'd set up his same furniture and hung familiar pieces. The first month, he kept asking, "What the hell am I doing here?" He stayed in his apartment and socialized only during meal times.

Even though I typed and laminated a new TV channel chart for him, orienting him to new stations was a challenge. He kept asking why he couldn't get the Philadelphia news. "It's all Boston up here!" he bellowed. He thought he could be on the other side of the earth because the street names and towns sounded foreign to him.

At age eighty-eight, Dad had to adapt and develop a new routine. It took a couple of months. Now he leaves for breakfast at seven a.m. and often doesn't return to his apartment until after dinner. He likes being served nutritious meals in a bright dining room with linens. He's improved the range of motion of his arms from morning exercise class.

Dad has made friends with other residents and staff who laugh at his wisecracks and tolerate his strong opinions. That doesn't surprise me because he's always preferred the company of others to being alone. He participates in Bingo, brain games ("I knew all the answers," he tells me), discussion groups, and sing-alongs. He strives to stay mentally alert and, thank goodness, he is.

He claims a favorite rocking chair on the sunny side of the porch, where he watches people come and go. Sometimes he dozes there. He carps about the high school marching band making a ruckus across the street, but I know he secretly appreciates the sound of life.

There isn't the same sense of happy for Dad and his fellow residents who have suffered loss. However, he is content. He is cared for. He is near family. Most importantly, he is safe.

I no longer have the six-hour drive to the bayside home where my parents retired. Instead of filling the freezer with single-serving meals, I fill Dad's pill sorter every week.

I don't worry about him falling with no one around to notice he's missing or sick. I no longer feel sad hanging up the phone from our daily calls knowing he was alone and trying to convince me he was okay when I heard the melancholy in his voice. Now when the phone rings, his voice is lighter. I can be by his side in ten minutes.

I am that woman now. The one who drives him to appointments and helps him answer questions at the doctor's office. The one who smiles at the bank teller when Dad tells the same joke. The one the waitress recognizes at the local café where Dad and I go for breakfast and watch small propeller planes take off and land. The one who reorders his meds, does his laundry, and picks up Gillette razors at CVS. The one who changes batteries, reviews the mail with him, and stocks his fridge with small water bottles because they're easier for him to handle than the large ones.

I'm the one who hears the same stories of his youth and his wartime. The one with whom he discusses politics, sports, and current events. The one who listens while he reminisces about Mom and his mother when he comes to my house for Sunday dinner of Italian meatballs, sausage, and rigatoni.

I am the woman he greets with a smile and leans forward to receive a kiss. The one he always thanks, and to whom he frequently says, "You look pretty, honey."

I am his caregiver, his friend, his chauffeur, his advisor, his confidante. I am that woman who leaves his apartment with a smile and sometimes a tear.

My role scares me and humbles me. I try not to worry about what the future holds, to take it one day at a time. I'm doing the best I can at a job that never occurred to me—a job that requires patience and energy but whose unexpected reward is abundant love.

Dad's fellow residents say to me, "Your father's a lucky man."
I tell them, "I'm the lucky one."
I am that woman.

Heart OF THE HOME

The Front Porch

My heart fluttered when my husband turned the corner in our minivan. I was eager to show our young daughters the house in Drexel Hill, Pennsylvania where I grew up. As we drove closer, tears filled my eyes and a lump formed in my throat.

"Oh, my God," I said softly, hand to chest. "Here it is."

The front porch of our two-story stone Colonial was the most restful retreat in the world, especially in the summertime. My sisters, brother, and I would fight for a seat on the squeaky glider. From that spot, we'd watch neighborhood kids ride bikes, play street hockey and basketball, or just wait for friends and relatives. At night, we'd stargaze or huddle with Dad during rainstorms. He taught us to count between the lightning and the thunder to calculate how far the storm was from our house.

Flanked by dogwood trees but with nothing to obscure our view, our porch was the perfect spot to witness neighborhood happenings.

"Mr. Cavalli is sealing his driveway again," I'd say, taking a break from reading. Every July, tall and slim Mr. Cavalli stood across the street with several five-gallon containers of tar, methodically moving a long squeegee from the back of his driveway to the front. All of our neighbors kept their houses and gardens in tiptop shape. You never saw clutter on anyone's property.

My favorite time on the porch was between four o'clock and four-thirty, waiting for Dad to come home from work. On summer days, I'd leap off the glider, open the front door, and yell, "Mom, Dad's home!" She'd rush out, tugging her shirt down, smile, and wave at the handsome guys in Dad's car pool.

In my teens, I'd linger on the porch, anticipating a good night kiss at the end of a date. But there was never more than a peck, because between the porch light and the street light opposite our house, the place was lit up like Fenway Park. On several Sunday mornings Dad said: "You forgot to turn off the porch light last night. What, do you think I have stock in the electric company?"

At twenty-four I moved out, yet with each visit home my heartbeat quickened when approaching the front door. Crossing the threshold, I was instantly comforted by the familiar sights and smells of home: the eagle door knocker, the umbrella stand and antique wooden sconce in the hallway, and the aromas from my mother's Italian cooking wafting from the kitchen, beckoning me into the heart of the home.

The house number in black script (Eight O Four) that Mom bought long ago remained nailed to the horizontal trim of the porch. Yes, this was the house, but someone might as well have punched me in the gut. The current owners had let the place go, and I barely recognized it. The driveway looked like a used-car lot, with rusty, dented vehicles parked too tightly on the small stretch of concrete. Stacks of firewood and broken furniture on the porch were visible behind the overgrown bushes that Dad had proudly trimmed long ago. Mom's flower boxes had vanished. The paint was peeling. My family home had become the eyesore on the block, and I regretted showing it to my daughters.

I wiped away the tears, turned to my husband, and said, "Keep driving."

Originally published in the Boston Globe *as* "Seeing Is Disbelieving," *December 20, 2015.*

The Heart-Attack Couch

First Apartment

Finally on my own. One hundred miles from home in northern New Jersey. The first piece of furniture I buy is a puffy Laura Ashley couch in a blue floral pattern. The deliverymen cannot maneuver it up the stairs to my garden apartment, so they tie a thick rope around it and hoist it to the second-story porch. Dad leans over the railing and grabs one stuffed arm. Later he confesses he thought he'd suffer a heart attack bending over holding on to that much weight. The couch is the centerpiece of my apartment filled with hand-me-downs and yard sale finds. I often fall asleep there watching *Dynasty* on a twelve-inch black-and-white television.

Second Apartment

Additional 275 miles farther north. The relocation company delivers my couch to the first-floor apartment in an expansive Colonial on Main Street in northeastern Massachusetts. I position the couch on an angle opposite the fireplace, which never crackles with cozy ambience because I dare not risk a back draft with the fussy homeowner living on the other side of the wall. Dates with my future husband usually end on the couch with the lights turned down low.

First Home

Single and living together. The couch's next stop is our southern-exposure living room two exits down the highway. When Dad arrives after the seven-hour drive, he announces, "I'm going to rest on the heart-attack couch." I pose for a photo on it with an engagement ring, holding a bouquet of red roses. A couple years later, I shuffle to the couch in the wee hours of morning to nurse the babies. Hubby and I cuddle with our daughters under an afghan and sing lullabies. One year's Christmas card shows the darlings in colorful Gymboree dresses seated on it with their feet barely reaching the edge of the seat cushion. I read cardboard picture books to them and listen as they point and say new words.

Second Home

Bigger house six miles from the first. The couch goes in the formal living room. When the print fades, I opt for a custom slipcover in a green paisley fabric. In the stillness of this room, my daughters and I review their report cards. After dinner, they read literature assigned by their teachers. I soothe them with a hug when one cries about not making the volleyball team and the other despairs over acne. On wintry Sunday afternoons, I read under a soft yellow blanket or gaze out the windows to watch snow fall. I talk on the phone with my sisters and finalize the details of our parents' fiftieth anniversary party. I hear the news of my parents' deteriorating health and make plans to travel, first for Dad's heart surgery and, three years later, for Mom's heart surgery.

Someone Else's Home

Time for a change. Twenty-nine years later, the still-comfy lounger used for quiet moments of reflection and conversation outlasts my expectations. After my daughters go to college, I transform the sitting room into a writing room with a sleek new sofa, desk, bookcase, and leather reading chair. I decide to relocate the old couch again, but the oversized family fixture will not fit down the basement stairs. Within hours of posting an ad online, my first piece of furniture sells for 150 dollars. The truck pulls out of the driveway and I don't look back.

The Guest Room

Entering the guest room in my father's house is like taking a sedative. It instantly calms me, particularly after the six-hour drive from my home in Massachusetts.

After the reunion hugs and kisses, I carry my bags into the cozy room and set my weekender onto the wooden luggage rack at the foot of the bed. When Mom bought the rack years prior, I thought, *Who's going to use this?*

As I unpack, I scan the room to make sure nothing changed. I kick off my shoes and push them under the side chair. I lay my make-up case, jewelry, and hairbrush on the maple dresser. Mom used to thoughtfully place a tray there for my personal items. I miss that gentle act of hospitality from her.

The guest room has offered me different refuge over the years. I first stayed here with my husband when we visited with our young daughters, who would sleep upstairs. Then I occupied the room alone when I helped Dad after his heart bypass operation and again after Mom's stroke. I enjoyed reciprocating as caregiver, chef, and housekeeper. After those busy days, I found supreme comfort in the guest bed, collapsing from fatigue with an *ahhh*. It wasn't how I'd imagined finally getting my own room, but I appreciated it all the same.

My father still surprises me in the evening, when I enter the temporary sanctuary after an island-filled day of walking, shopping, and gardening, to discover that he had turned down the bed for me. His tender act of love moves me. My chest softens.

I sleep soundly in this guest room. Sometimes the wind howls and sometimes the rain pings the rooftop. Once in a while I hear the awning or our American flag flapping against the wind. Other times I detect the faint drum of traffic heading for the bridge a few blocks away. All these rhythmic sounds of the island lull me into a peaceful slumber.

The deep muffle of Dad's footsteps from above gives me the sense that Father Protector shields me. Yet, somehow I never hear him tiptoe down the stairs and open the front door to claim his newspaper before sunrise, as he takes care not to disturb me. When I do awake, my body is fully rested, with nary an ache, and my skin glows a pinkish hue.

On a recent drive back home, I decided to refurnish my own guest room. Inspired by Long Beach Island, I styled the room with new curtains and a coverlet in the blue, green, and sand colors of the island. A beach-chair lamp, starfish against the windowpanes, and a bowl of golden beige stones collected from the bay beach in Surf City add to the theme.

Since Mom passed away and Dad no longer travels far, this cozy nook reminds me of my home away from home.

My Bout with Lyme Disease

I hadn't slept well for several nights leading up to that Sunday morning. Sprawled on the couch the night before with the TV on, I tossed and turned, threw the blanket off, put it back on, sipped water, popped Tylenol, sipped more water, and darted back and forth to the bathroom. I knew I had a fever but never bothered to check how high it was.

By six o'clock in the morning, barely able to move, I lugged my body up the stairs and climbed into bed, where I lay like a boulder on the mattress. At ten a.m., I dragged myself off the bed, wobbled back and forth, then leaned on the doorframe. A feeble cry of "Good morning?" down the stairs went unanswered. I craved orange juice. Too weak to make it to the kitchen on my own, I reasoned a shower would wake me up. That's when the nightmare started.

I turned my back to the hot spray, lathered up, and opened my eyes to find the shower tiles lifting off the wall and the grout lines spinning diagonally. Despite my lightheadedness, I thought, No, this is fine, I can go on. But I heard another voice frantically say, Joyce, stop, you're going to faint.

I put my hands on the slippery side wall, slowly pivoted, and turned off the faucet. Then I opened the glass shower door and yelled for my husband, Gary. Oh dear, he'd probably be tinkering in the garage or yard and wouldn't hear me. While

I stood still as a statue, afraid to move, my savior appeared in front of me.

"I feel dizzy," I said.

"Okay," Gary said, reaching his hands to me, palms up. "Grab my arms."

My hands grabbed his elbows and we stood forearm to forearm. The next thing I knew I was on the shower floor with Gary holding me under my armpits.

"Did I just faint?"

"Yeah," he said, struggling, his right foot in the shower. "Can you get up?"

"I think so," I said, slowly rising with his help.

"Do you think you can step out?"

I wobbled, stepped out of the shower, and then everything faded to black.

"Did I faint again?"

"Yeah," he said, elbowing the door open wide while kicking the cotton bath mat away.

I heard my teenage daughter in the master bedroom saying, "One one six," our house number.

"An ambulance is on the way," said Gary.

"No. I don't need an ambulance," I protested, naked and dripping wet, on all fours, crawling to the toilet to vomit.

"Yes, you do, Joyce. They're coming," he insisted.

Before I knew it, heavy footsteps on the stairs grew closer. Commotion. Scuffle. I sensed someone large standing in front of me. The bathroom felt crowded. They asked me a few questions and took my blood pressure. I never saw the paramedics' faces, choosing to keep my eyes closed the moment they arrived. I didn't want to give this drama a movie frame.

"Okay, we're going to strap you onto this chair and take you downstairs into the ambulance. Are you ready?"

Straps, heavy boots on the tile floor (I hope the tiles don't crack from all the weight), shuffling, buckles clicking. Clunk, clunk, clunk down the stairs. (Note to self: wash stairs when you get home this afternoon.)

The misting rain gave me goose bumps, yet the clean, June-morning air refreshed me compared to the humid, crowded bathroom. Clunk, clunk, clunk down the steps outside. In the driveway, they lowered the back of the transfer seat flat and slid me into the ambulance.

They took my blood pressure again and that's when I knew something was seriously wrong. Either they didn't announce the first reading in the bathroom or I didn't hear it. This time I heard it. Fifty-seven over thirty-eight. Holy cow! Fifty-seven! I'm half dead! Fifty-seven. That's the year of my birth.

While Gary sat in the front seat of the ambulance, the paramedic kept poking the inside of my elbow, searching for a vein with his warm, fleshy hands.

"Joyce, I notice you have a big garden. Do you spend a lot of time gardening?"

"Not as much as I used to. Just some weeding now and then." Who was I kidding? It dawned on me that he must be thinking about Lyme disease, but neither of us mentioned those words. I knew Lyme disease could be fatal.

"I have small veins. They're always hard to find. Try over here," I motioned to the outer edge of my arm. Reaching for the paramedic's hand, my hand found his firm belly instead and I discovered how much he likes burgers and beer.

After several minutes of unsuccessful attempts to find a vein, we left for the hospital. A roller coaster of bumps and swerves along with the whoop-whoop of the sirens at every intersection woke me from my half slumber. Wait a minute, those sirens whoop-whooped for me. Traffic stopped for me.

I visualized the fifteen-minute route to the hospital and knew when we'd arrived at the emergency entrance. Scuffle, car doors opening and closing, metal clanging, Gary's voice, cool breeze, bang on the concrete, bumpy ride, squeaky wheels, and automatic doors sliding open, until, finally, a flat, smooth hospital floor.

"Okay, Joyce. Open your eyes, please." A handsome ER doctor in a white coat stood over me asking questions while a phlebotomist inserted an IV and someone else took my vital signs.

"Does your head hurt?"

"No."

"Does your neck hurt?"

"No."

"Does your throat hurt?"

"No."

"Does this hurt?" he asked, pressing his hands into my right side, above my liver.

"No."

"Does anything hurt?"

"My back."

"Have you been out of the country recently?"

"No."

"You haven't taken any trips?"

"No."

"Have you eaten at any restaurants in the last few days?"

"No."

"No shellfish? No restaurants at all?"

"No. No shellfish. I ate at an Italian restaurant about a week ago." Words trickled out like a movie track with damaged sound effects.

"Has she been disoriented lately?" he asked Gary.

"No. She drove into Boston yesterday and took a class,"

Gary said proudly. "She's really a healthy person. She's the best eater I know. She practices yoga several times a week and walks regularly. She's never sick."

At one point, a male nurse with a slight build in plain blue scrubs shuffled his feet near the gurney but wouldn't provide details. Then he acquiesced and said quietly, "They think it might be sepsis."

"Sepsis!" I said. "I'll be dead by tomorrow." I knew people who died of sepsis within a couple of days of being diagnosed. Suddenly, I feared for my life. I felt compelled to relay to Gary maternal instructions about what to say to our daughters the rest of their lives, but I couldn't think fast enough, much less form the words. How would he handle their graduations, weddings, and other important milestones without me? What pearls of wisdom could he offer them that they would never hear from their mother?

After an hour or so of more diagnostics, the doctor said he was admitting me.

"Admitting me?" Wow, this was serious. The only time in my life I was hospitalized was to give birth. "What for?" I asked.

"Your body is in shock. Your blood pressure is severely low, your temp is too high, and we need to run more tests."

I closed my eyes to the bright lights, held Gary's hand, and prayed.

Within the next two days, still sleepless, my psoriatic arthritis flared up, my skin yellowed due to an inflamed liver, pink blotches appeared on random parts of my body, and I developed palsy in my eyelids. My temperature remained high, my liver enzymes were off the chart, and my white and red blood cell counts bounced up and down.

Finally, a diagnosis of Lyme disease. A bouquet of thick plastic bags containing various colored liquids hung above my bed and, by Tuesday night, I started to feel better.

I took Doxycycline for two months, which killed my appetite because of its metallic aftertaste. I had to stay out of the sun and had no energy anyway. So I spent most of the summer reading on the screened porch twenty yards from the garden where, presumably, I contracted the disease.

Can you imagine a tick the size of a period on this page, something I never felt or saw, could do so much damage? It was unusual to find myself in the vulnerable situation of needing medical attention after being blessed with good health for many years. I reluctantly gave myself over to the care of others. In doing so, I discovered that mothers aren't the only people who can make the hurt go away.

When I think of how I felt my life hanging in the balance, I am thankful to have been caught, diagnosed early, and restored to good health.

Note: According to my infectious disease doctor, high fevers shouldn't happen in June. If you have one and are experiencing flu-like symptoms, get to the doctor immediately and ask to be tested for Lyme disease. If your dog is unusually lethargic, get him checked, too. Finally, cover yourself when gardening and examine every part of your body before showering; have a family member check your back and scalp.

Firefighters to the Rescue

My daughter rapped on the bathroom door while I was in the shower.

"Mom, get out!"

She opened the door a crack and yelled, "The carbon monoxide detector is beeping. I called the fire department. They're on their way. We have to get out of the house. Hurry up!"

With my hair full of suds, I turned off the faucet and grabbed a towel. I quickly patted dry and pulled on sweatpants and a sweatshirt. Then I went downstairs, unlocked the front door, grabbed a coat and hat, stepped into boots, and followed my daughter out the back door.

On that sunny, January morning, we waited for the firefighters to arrive in the slippery driveway among five-foot snow banks. My gut told me the house was fine but with the brutal winter we'd been having, I couldn't have known for sure.

"Remember when they came on Christmas Eve a few years ago?" said Kristin, laughing. The smoke detector had gone off when I opened the oven door and a plume of blue smoke escaped from the beef tenderloin. The piercing, persistent alarm drowned out holiday music as we laughed and scrambled to open windows to the snowy wonderland while waiting for the firefighters.

"Oh yeah. That was funny. We gave the neighbors a show, didn't we?" I chuckled, thinking about the scene.

Several minutes later, a big red truck lumbered into our post-blizzard neighborhood (thankfully, without a siren this time). It parted the snow banks like a cherry's juice dripping down an ice cream sundae.

Three firefighters trod into the house and quickly ascertained that the carbon monoxide detector only had a low battery. I felt somewhat embarrassed that I hadn't taken the time to stop and check, but they were so good-natured about the situation.

On the way out of the front door, one guy asked if we'd cleared the fire hydrant on the edge of our property.

"We cleared it after the first storm," I said, "but we couldn't keep up after the blizzard."

"Let's get the shovels," he said to his buddies.

My daughter and I stayed outdoors and watched the men clear a path to the hydrant while they bantered amusedly. The brotherhood that often defines firefighters was on full display.

As the truck pulled away, I asked myself what it is about firefighters that people find so intriguing. I think it's the combination of their virility and humility. Thanks, guys.

Letter to a Bath

Dear Bath,

The last time I saw you, you comforted me after I experienced a severe allergic reaction to new draperies that were installed in my family room. How was I to know the fabric had some kind of protective coating on it?

Within minutes, I was scratching my arms. Two hours later, I lay in bed before throwing the covers off me. An itching frenzy overtook my face, neck, chest, and legs. I felt as if I'd been attacked by a swarm of mosquitoes.

When I looked in the bathroom mirror, I was horrified to see my skin covered with pink bumps of all shapes and sizes. The rash covered my entire body, including my scalp. I jittered in pain, wishing I could peel off my skin.

Hubby dashed out to the pharmacy and bought Benadryl and Aveeno oatmeal bath treatment to soothe my dermal fury until I could see a doctor the next day and get a prescription. I soaked in your warm and curative waters and felt relief. We met again over the following two days. In all, I'd missed three days of work.

Bath, I am thankful for your healing power. As you know, I'm basically a shower girl, but I appreciate you being there in my time of need.

Sincerely,
Sensitive Skin

P.S. The draperies were removed the next day.

Yard Sale to Salvage Yard

My mother found an iron bed at a yard sale. She thought that if we painted it white, it would look nice with my Laura Ashley comforter and shams. It did, but when I relocated from one apartment to another, the mover used a rubber mallet to fit a side rail into the dovetail slot, and the piece broke off, rendering the bedframe useless. So I used the headboard only. I don't remember what happened to the rails and footboard.

Once married with new furniture, I relegated the headboard to the garage. When my husband and I moved to our current home, I decided to "plant" it in the garden, thinking it would make an interesting visual among the perennials.

Then the garden got a major cleaning and I decided to retire the rusted piece. Instead of putting it to the curb, I took it to a salvage yard, where I backed my car into an oversized, gritty garage.

"We'll weigh it," said the guy who removed it. "Go over to the office after you park your car outside."

I lifted my summer maxi skirt and tiptoed in wedge sandals across the dirt lot into the dark and dingy office.

"Are you the white Acura?" asked the woman behind the counter.

"That's me."

"There's your cash."

"Wow! Two dollars and ten cents."

"Twenty-eight pounds of light iron. Seven-and-a-half cents a pound. Thanks for recycling."

I bought an iced coffee on the way home.

On a Bicycle Built for Two

My mother decided we should enter a Fourth of July contest for the best decorated bike at our elementary school in suburban Philadelphia. Back in 1970, we owned a bicycle built for two.

Dad had bought the gold Schwinn, used, from a shop owner down the shore at the end of the prior summer season. No one else in the neighborhood had anything as unique, and kids would beg to ride it.

Using red, white, and blue crepe paper and small American flags, my younger sister, Alison, and cousin Mary decorated the bike. While they weaved the patriotic stripes through the spokes, Mom and Aunt Tootsie cobbled together an outfit for the two girls to wear. The moms fashioned the idea of a Gay Nineties (that's 1890s) couple.

Alison wasn't too happy that she had to dress as the man in a seersucker jacket and Styrofoam hat. Petite Mary giggled while my aunt stuffed her top with tissue paper. Mary had to lift the hem of her skirt in order to walk and pedal from the back seat.

Together, the young cousins road that festive two-seater to Drexel Hill Elementary, paraded in front of the judges, and won first place. I think they got a blue ribbon attached to the handlebars.

You couldn't help but smile, seeing that bike on the road, or better yet, riding it. Of course, the rider in front had the tougher job pedaling.

Ten years later, my parents took the bike to Long Beach Island, where they'd bought a cottage. I can still see Mom and Dad gliding down the street together. Dad huffed and puffed in front while Mom stuck her legs out and yelled, "Whee!" as if she hadn't a care in the world. That's the feeling you got when riding our bicycle built for two.

Kitchen Bouquet

"Flowers for me?" I asked one Saturday morning.

"They were on the list," my husband called from the basement.

"On the list?"

"You wrote 'kitchen bouquet' on the grocery list."

I burst out laughing.

"I meant Kitchen Bouquet, the seasoning for the turkey gravy."

"Oh. I thought it was odd to see it written there. I figured you wanted flowers for Thanksgiving."

I can't complain. Mr. MOTM has done the grocery shopping every week for our entire marriage. Because he always sticks to the list, our Thanksgiving table will be adorned with colorful blooms.

Mrs. Fix-It

I returned from my morning walk on Sunday and saw hubby's leg hanging out of the trunk of a car. He was trying to replace the lightbulb in the rear window of our daughter's Hyundai.

"Need some help?" I asked, noticing various tools strewn on the trunk floor.

"Yeah, climb onto the back seat and hold the unit steady while I try to screw the bulb in place," he said.

We weren't having success. It's not a straight-on fit. You have to insert the bulb through a small opening in a metal plate, angle it over, and then turn it clockwise to snap into place. Not an easy feat for man hands.

"Let me try," I said.

I eased into the trunk, rear end first, lay down and assessed the situation with an L. L. Bean Trailblazer Headlamp. My neck muscles strained, so I rolled the plastic bottle of windshield wiper fluid under my neck for support.

I fiddled and jiggled with my right (dominant) hand. Each time, the bulb fell and I'd get a glimpse of fall foliage through that hole the size of a quarter.

Then I clamped the unit between the forefinger and middle finger of my left hand. That turned out to be the winning maneuver.

"I think I did it. I don't see the sky."

"All right!" said my husband. "Let's see if it works." I may have detected a slight surprise in his voice.

I climbed out of the car and witnessed the orange flash when hubby pressed the brake pedal.

As I walked toward the house, I heard him say, "Not bad, only twelve tools."

"And all you needed was a woman," I replied, strolling confidently down the driveway.

Showering Outdoors

There's nothing like taking a shower outdoors. I remember my first time. I was a preteen, standing in a stall at the house of a family friend in Beach Haven, thinking the sensation was the coolest thing ever.

When my parents bought their home on Long Beach Island, an outdoor shower became the norm after a day at the beach. One by one, family members and friends took their turn under the spray. Then we'd meet on the deck and enjoy wine and cheese.

Those days have passed. However, showering outdoors is one of the many things I still look forward to when visiting Dad on the island. A cool cascade refreshes me after a day of sweat and salt water. Droplets of water pinging on the deck boards and sunlight cutting through the top of the shower stall put me in a near-meditative state. Washing with pear soap and coconut shampoo is a treat. Even getting dressed in the adjoining stall is liberating—unless you prefer to exit the shower wrapped in a towel only, and then it's really liberating. It's so much better walking out into a summer breeze instead of a humid bathroom after a shower.

After hanging my towel on the clothesline, I comb out my hair and let the loose strands blow in the breeze.

Showering outdoors means you needn't worry about a bath

mat, slipping on the wooden deck boards, hair in the drain, or mildew accumulating. Just leave the shower door open and let Mother Nature dry it clean.

I'd shower outdoors every day if I could, but living in New England prohibits me from that indulgence.

Shake the Toilet

My father had a new toilet installed in his house and it triggered a vivid childhood memory.

We'd all just turned off the lights and settled into bed. You know the stillness that descends on the home when everyone gets under the covers in darkness—the one where you can almost hear the house sigh, lulling you into slumber?

Well, that night, the sound of silence was interrupted by a noise coming from the bathroom. I remember it as a hum. Maybe you'd call it a rattle or a gurgle or a bubbling. Whatever the sound, it wasn't inhibiting my ability to drift, but apparently the cacophony annoyed my father. Dad must have just collapsed onto the mattress when he asked his ten-year-old, whose bed was closest to the bathroom, to stop the annoyance emanating from the upstairs john.

"Joyce, go shake the toilet," Dad said.

I was flummoxed by Dad's direction. Shake the toilet? I pulled back my covers and dutifully padded to the bathroom. With the toilet seat up, I gazed down through half-shut eyes and noticed the water rippling around the edge of the bowl. I pondered how to shake a toilet. Don't you shake something like a snow globe?

I squatted and placed my hands on each side of the porcelain throne and attempted to shake it side to side. The bowl wouldn't budge. The gurgling continued. I remained in a squat position and considered my next step.

"It won't move," I called to Dad.

Then I heard him laughing. I peered out of the door and had a straight-line view into my parents' bedroom. There I saw Dad lying on the edge of the bed, his head craned toward me with one hand on the floor holding him from completely falling over with laughter.

Such a serious child, I couldn't understand the humor.

"Joyce," he said, still chuckling. "When I said shake the toilet, I meant shake the handle."

"Oh," I said, slowly rising.

"Shake the handle."

"You mean jiggle the handle?"

"Yes, yes! Jiggle the handle."

"Okay."

So I jiggled the handle because of course you can't shake a toilet handle that's secured to the tank just like you can't shake a toilet bowl that's screwed into a tile floor.

I waited for the gurgling to subside. Leaving the quieted bathroom, I noticed Dad raise his hand to forehead and roll onto his back, still chuckling. He must have slept well that night.

Flying from the Nest

My college graduate is moving out. She's been preparing me for her flight from the nest for a while now. I'm happy for her and sad to see her go even though when she's home, you'd barely know it because she's quiet and independent. She's the calming influence and voice of reason in our family.

I thought I'd prepared my mother when announcing my move but she was shocked. She finally came around to accepting me living 100 miles away, knowing I'd be near an aunt and uncle.

Mom helped me furnish my first apartment in garage sale chic. She scored a maple side chair and covered it with corduroy cushions, a dining table and chairs, and a vanity that she helped me strip and stain in the back yard of the beach house. Those refurbished pieces looked great with the new bed and dresser Mom bought me.

Thirty-four years later, my daughter sanded and painted that same dresser (which is still in great shape). White paint and updated hardware made it new again for her first apartment. Mom would have been glad.

I find myself eager to purchase linens and things for my daughter and offer her items from our furniture cemetery, just like Mom did for me.

"How about this lamp?" I ask, lifting it from an old end table in the basement.

"No, thanks."

"Are you sure?"

"Mom . . . my apartment!"

Right. Her apartment. Her tastes. She's on her way and I feel good knowing she has a piece of me with her. And she's only twenty-five miles away.

An Artificial Christmas Tree

Never thought I'd do it—buy an artificial Christmas tree. I know, I know, the real ones smell great. So do scented balsam candles.

I'm tired of sweeping the needles, seeing branches droop, crouching on the floor to water the base, and invariably wetting the tree skirt.

No matter how many times we carried the tree in and out of the house wrapped in a sheet of plastic, needles found their way into a closet, grout line, windowsill, curtain hem, and baseboard edge. The following spring I'd find green slivers in yet another crevice.

In the early days of married life, Mr. MOTM and I would make a day of driving to a Christmas tree farm and enjoy walking through rows of fir, spruce, and balsam on a cold November afternoon to tag a tree. We'd return a few weeks later and take pride in chopping it down ourselves.

Then came the stage when our toddler daughters joined us on the hunt and scurried through aisles of evergreen shouting, "The biggest one, Daddy!"

In following years, on frigid December days, we three girls would wait in the heated minivan while Mr. MOTM took all of a minute at a local, muddy nursery before emerging in front of the headlights with his hand held on the trunk of the tree.

He'd stand next to it and wordlessly give me a blank stare. I'd nod and give him a thumbs up.

Before we knew it, our daughters got their driver's licenses and decided it would be an adventure to select a tree on their own. They'd come home all smiles and giggles, with their find tied to the roof of the SUV. Their father would remove the tree and lean it against the garage door before lugging it indoors a day or two later.

Once the girls went to college, hubby would simply arrive home with a smaller tree, without my knowing. "Fine," I'd say, and the two of us would decorate it—he, the lights and me, the garland and ornaments—before our darlings returned to the nest for semester break.

Somehow, I'm the one who always undresses the tree. Maybe because, even though I love a lighted tree (white lights only!), particularly in early morning, I'm ready to see the thing gone two days after Christmas. I'd had enough of sweeping and vacuuming the greenery that covered the floor with the slightest touch of a branch.

So last year, although the rest of my family still preferred a real tree, Mr. MOTM admitted he was tired of the mess, too. We shopped for an artificial tree the day after Christmas and found one discounted at seventy-five percent off. Lights included. Bingo!

We assembled the yuletide attraction easily and quickly and like it more than we thought. I hope it'll be as easy storing the tree back in its box as it was putting it together. All I know is I won't have to reach for a broom or vacuum cleaner.

Minimizing with My Sisters

Why is it easier to see what changes should be done in other people's houses than in your own? We live with the same mundane objects day after day even if we don't use them. The problem is that if you have the space, things accumulate.

My husband and daughters will tell you how organized our house is and how quick I am to toss stuff in the trash or recycle bin. They've heard my mantra "less is more" many times. I can't stand clutter. Everything must be in its proper place. Clean, clear surfaces relax me.

Yet when my sister visited last weekend, she saw room for even more minimizing. Alison has become obsessive compulsive since she downsized. She eliminated excess items from her former home and thinks our sister Lynne and I should do the same. The difference is that we still live in our big houses with lots of storage space while she's nesting in a cute little apartment.

"What's with all the large serving platters? Who's coming?" Alison asked.

I chuckled. True, I've never hosted dozens of family members for holiday meals the way my mother and aunts did when all the relatives lived close by.

"What about this salad spinner? Do you ever use it?"

"No."

"Throw it out."

I dutifully complied while our sister Lynne sipped wine at the kitchen table and laughed, too. She'd been through this process with Alison the previous month when instructed to excavate the two large bushes flanking her porch steps. Alison also convinced Lynne to relocate an antique curio cabinet from the basement to the kitchen. Together they cleaned and filled it with meaningful gifts. Lynne admittedly likes both updates.

While I sorted and stacked plastic ware ("How many leftover containers do you need?"), Alison opened the pantry closet and lined up boxes of crackers and pasta. They looked fine to me but she wanted all the labels facing the same direction.

During the course of the weekend, I noticed other changes while moving about the house without her. She had pushed the couch on the screened-in porch on a diagonal. I admit it looks better. She covered the dirt on the plant in the powder room with small shells. "Your guests don't want to see dirt," she said.

I miss my sisters who live out of state. We only see one another a couple of times a year. So when they come to my house, I'm eager to let them add their touches here and there. It makes me feel more connected to them.

Before leaving for the airport, Alison put her coffee cup down, looked at Lynne and me, and said, "Do we have time to tackle that linen closet?" She thinks I have more curtains, tablecloths, and cotton napkins than I need. She's probably right.

"No, but I'll leave something else for you to organize on your next visit."

Upon returning home, I thinned out that closet. However, I did move the antique chair in the family room back two feet to its original spot.

Food
IS LOVE

Biscotti for My Accountant

For more than twenty years, my accountant has been coming to the house to collect tax documents and discuss the year's filing. We're the only house call he makes because he likes returning to his hometown to see what's changed. And sample my biscotti.

I serve the delicious Italian treats with coffee, and we discuss our children and the year's milestones. After our meeting, Jim leaves with a bag of biscotti, which he tells me he dips into on his drive home. At seventy-three, his private practice is thriving and he needs to whittle down his client list, but he assures my husband and me that he'll continue to be our accountant—as long as biscotti are served.

Baking relaxes me. The subtle, buttery aroma wafting through my kitchen is comforting. Bring biscotti to a friend. It makes a memorable gift.

Mix a stick of softened, unsalted butter and ¾ cup of sugar until fluffy. Whisk in two eggs and 1 TB vanilla extract. Add 2 cups flour, 1½ tsp baking powder, ½ tsp salt, and mix with a wooden spoon.

Optional: add 1 cup of chopped walnuts. Sometimes I divide the batter and make half plain and half with nuts. You can substitute pistachios or almonds but, in my experience, the almond loaves don't slice as well.

Flour your fingertips and mold two loaves approximately 12" long and 4" wide onto a baking sheet. Bake at 325 degrees for 25 minutes until light golden brown.

Cool for 5 minutes.

Transfer to a cutting board and use a bread knife to cut ½-inch-thick diagonal slices. Return to baking sheet and bake for 10 minutes or until they are dry and nicely browned.

Biscotti means "twice baked" in Italian, but this is where I deviate from the recipe. Instead of baking again, I put the sheet on the lowest rack and turn the oven to broil to lightly toast each side of the biscotti. Toasting this way is faster, but you have to watch closely to make sure they don't burn.

Let cool.

Sometimes I dip one side of the biscotti into melted dark chocolate. Keep on the cooling rack and stick in the freezer for 5 minutes until the chocolate hardens.

Biscotti freeze well.

Mangia!

Texas Caviar

In the spirit of healthy eating, here's a recipe everyone will enjoy. It makes a great appetizer during football season and also pairs well with fish. We also call this dish "Confetti."

1 can black-eyed peas
1 can black beans
1 can shoepeg white corn
½ orange pepper, diced
½ red pepper, diced
½ red onion, diced
3-4 celery stalks, diced

Dressing
1/3 cup vegetable oil
1/3 cup cider vinegar
1 TB sugar

Rinse beans and corn. Dice vegetables very small. Combine in a large bowl. Pour dressing and toss gently.

Serve with Tostitos scoops or your favorite chip. With or without the dressing, you'll get addicted. Mangia!

Top 10 Food Memories

When someone asks about my favorite food, I conjure up a memory. Where was I? Who was I with? What was the occasion? How did I feel? The food itself may or may not have been rated "the best" by a discerning critic, but the setting and circumstances made it taste like the best ever to me.

Here are ten of my happiest food memories.

French onion soup in Old Montreal. Hubby (then boyfriend) and I spent an afternoon ice-skating at the Olympic Park. I'd fallen and injured my right elbow. That night, we found a romantic restaurant on the corner of a cobblestone street and sat at a table by the window. I had to use my left hand to spoon the flavorful soup.

Halibut in Kennebunkport, Maine. After cocktails on the porch of Cape Arundel Inn, overlooking the ocean, this delectable white fish was prepared to perfection.

Hot dog in Freeport, Bahamas. At the end of a family vacation at the Westin Lucaya, we noticed a guy serving barbecued hot dogs at one end of the beach. The sun, sand, music, and breeze made the hot dog taste yummy.

Sausage and pepper sandwich at the Boston Garden. While waiting for the Celine Dion concert to begin, I had a hankering and that sandwich hit the spot like no other time I can remember.

French fries in Nantucket. Hubby and I had parked our bikes outside the West End restaurant following a sunny afternoon on nearby Madaket Beach. The basket of salty goodness complemented our ice-cold drinks while we sat at the bar.

Yogurt parfait in Portland, Maine. I counted twelve different pieces of fruit served atop granola and yogurt at Becky's Diner on the waterfront. When I raved about the luscious treat to our server, she told me the parfait actually has a cult following.

Croissants in Ottawa. I first visited the capital of Canada on a business trip in 1984. Arriving at the Westin late at night, tired and hungry, I ordered room service of tea and croissants. When the tray arrived, I savored every buttery morsel while looking out at the brightly lit Rideau Canal from my twenty-first story window.

Granola on Martha's Vineyard. One of the many perks to attending a writer's retreat on the island was the fabulous granola. I mixed it with berries and yogurt for a great start to a day of creativity.

Lasagna in San Diego. I was thrilled to introduce my young daughters to my sweet Aunt Tootsie. She served her famous lasagna in a lovely dining room where we laughed with Uncle Freddie and told stories of my youth. No restaurant has ever come close to my aunt's signature Italian dish nor have I been able to replicate it.

Ravioli in West Philadelphia. In my youth, I loved running into Grandmom's kitchen to find her bent over the Formica table kneading dough and dropping dollops of ricotta onto each square. Then she'd carry the plate of heavenly ravioli into the dining room, where my family eagerly awaited her authentic Italian meal. It was pure love on a plate.

Of course everything I ate in Italy was memorable, but I'll stop here.

Sweet Tooth

Now I understand my mother's midlife craving. Often after dinner, I find myself repeating what she used to say: "I have a little sweet tooth."

I keep little pieces of Dove dark chocolate in a pretty candy dish in the dining room hutch. One piece satisfies me. Really. I don't hunger for a whole Snickers bar or piece of cake. Okay, I do enjoy a slice of pie occasionally.

Last night, when *Jeopardy!* started, I asked my daughter to bring me a piece of chocolate.

"You mean an antioxidant?" Mimicking me, she continued, "You know, dark chocolate is full of antioxidants and antioxidants are healthy for you."

As I savored my morsel, hubby piped up, "Sure, when you eat that, it's a healthy antioxidant. When we eat it, it's candy."

My First and Last St. Patrick's Day Dinner

A co-worker named Pegge invited me to her house one Sunday afternoon to celebrate St. Patrick's Day with her husband and two young sons.

"Come on over," she said. "We're having corned beef and cabbage."

"What's that?" I asked.

"You never had corned beef and cabbage?"

"No." I couldn't imagine what it even looked like.

"Well then, you definitely have to come over."

"I don't know . . ." How could I tell her it sounded awful?

"Oh c'mon! We'll be farting all night."

We burst into laughter. Pegge had so much energy you couldn't help but feel happy around her. I had nothing better to do and she knew it.

I was living alone in New Jersey in the early 1980s and had never eaten an Irish meal. My family had "gravy" on Sunday. That meant any shape of pasta (or macaroni, as we called it) with meatballs, sausage, and brasciole in marinara sauce. A loaf of crusty Italian bread, salad, and red wine for Mom and Dad completed our afternoon meal.

Pegge had other ideas that Sunday. She greeted me wearing a bright-green sweater. Shamrocks and leprechauns adorned the walls of the home where she chased after her toddlers.

Pegge ushered me into the kitchen and offered me beer, but I declined. (Never developed a taste for it.) I stopped short of wrinkling my nose. What was that smell? She proudly lifted the lid on a large pot and showed me the beef. What? Who cooks meat in boiling water?

By the time we sat down for dinner, I was still apprehensive about the food. The platter of corned beef looked so unappealing. It felt sacrilegious to be celebrating the Irish this way, on a Sunday no less. Give me spaghetti.

"Go on," said Pegge. "Help yourself. You'll love it," she said, spooning potatoes onto a plate for her son.

I took a small serving of the pink beef and the wilted cabbage. Slowly I cut the meat and then raised a forkful to my mouth while she watched in amusement.

"Mmmm," I said, nodding my head. It tasted salty but, to my surprise, I liked it more than I expected. Despite the savory meal, I haven't had a corned beef and cabbage dinner since that memorable day at Pegge's house.

Easy Pasta Recipe

If you're looking for an easy, nutritious dinner, try this. It's one of hubby's favorites: pasta with broccoli and kidney beans.

Saute broccoli florets in olive oil and butter with garlic. Drain dark-red kidney beans and toss in after broccoli is cooked. Be sure not to overcook the broccoli; you don't want it mushy.

Add drained pasta. I prefer radiatore with this dish, but cavatappi or rigatoni are good alternatives.

Gently stir. Add some red pepper flakes if you like a little zip.

Serve with freshly grated Parmigiano-Reggiano cheese.

And there you have the colors of the Italian flag.

Mangia!

A Lobster Tale

My family decided to end the summer with dinner on the beach. Mr. MOTM and daughters wanted pizza and I opted for a lobster roll at the nearby seafood shack.

We arranged our beach chairs in a semi-circle and placed the pizza box on a blanket. The cloudless sky, gentle breeze, low tide, and lack of crowds were perfect conditions for a relaxing family night out.

While the three of them reached for a pizza slice, I unwrapped a lobster roll chock full of meat. The bun was buttered and toasted just right. After the first bite, I declared it one of the tastiest sandwiches ever. I held my roll with both hands and prepared for a second bite when suddenly, out of nowhere, a big, black Labrador retriever shoved his nose over my shoulder. I screamed, jumped in my seat, and dropped the lobster roll into the sand, an inch from the edge of the blanket, meat side down.

"Are you kidding me?" I cried.

Seconds later, the owner called the dog that ran toward him while I sat staring at my ruined meal and cursing both the dog and owner.

My family and I laughed, but not too hard because I was still upset about losing my dinner.

I gingerly lifted the overturned roll and tried to reassemble the sandwich on my paper plate, but the damage was done. I even wiped sand off a chunk of lobster claw and chewed it.

"Gritty, huh, Mom?" said my daughter when she noticed the sour look on my face.

"Damn dog!" I said after spitting out the piece.

"There's still your cole slaw, Mom," said my other daughter, trying to sound hopeful.

They finished their pizza while I stuffed the sandy sandwich into a brown paper bag. I shoved the bag under the blanket when a couple of seagulls came toward me.

On the way home, Mr. MOTM suggested stopping for another lobster roll. I declined—not the same. My daughters occupied themselves in the back seat with their iPhone apps when one piped up: "Hey Mom, did you know today is National Dog Day?"

Spinach Balls

This yummy appetizer came from a Christmas party I attended years ago. I can't recall who gave me the recipe, but I've taken credit for it ever since.

- 1 10-oz. package of chopped spinach (thawed & drained)*
- 1 cup herb-seasoned stuffing
- 1 medium onion, chopped finely
- 3 beaten eggs
- 3 TB melted butter
- 1/4 cup Parmigiano-Reggiano cheese
- 1/2 tsp garlic powder
- 1/4 tsp thyme
- 1/4 tsp pepper

Take the frozen spinach out of the box the night before and let it drain. When you're ready to mix the ingredients, squeeze all the moisture out of the spinach.

Mix together. Roll into bite-size balls and place on a cookie sheet lined with parchment paper. Then freeze the tray for 15 minutes until the balls just harden.

Bake for 20 minutes at 350 degrees. Mangia!

Remembering Angelo

Angelo drove an ice cream truck that stopped in front of my house every night in spring and summer. I'd hear the familiar rumble coming down Stoneybrook Lane to its last stop on my street.

On the side of the big yellow truck, Angelo's name was painted on an angle in script. As it slowed, Angelo would ring his bell and cry out, "Lo, lo, lo!" That sent kids running indoors for change from their moms to buy ice cream, water ice, or candy.

Angelo wore a short-sleeve, button-down shirt and trousers every day, no matter what the temperature. He'd wipe the forehead of his balding head with a hanky and stuff it in his back pocket before placing his palms on the ledge of the large open window on the side of the truck.

Kids would clamor to state their order for a cold afternoon treat, nudging one another to get to the front of the line. Angelo patiently took each child's request and kept conversation to a minimum, only occasionally revealing his Italian accent.

I didn't want any sweets, though. I wanted the other treat Angelo sold stacked atop the refrigerated boxes that I spied over his left shoulder: a soft pretzel from South Philly.

If you've never had an authentic Philadelphia soft pretzel, you don't know what you're missing. The salted, doughy delight is slightly crunchy on the outside and soft on the inside. No other soft pretzel compares. If you grew up in the Philadelphia area, you don't bother eating any other kind.

The customary way to eat a soft pretzel is this: Hold the pretzel in the center between your thumb and middle finger and start with the rounded end. Then eat the other rounded end bite by bite, saving the best part for last, the knot. The knot is the thickest part of the pretzel that you slowly sink your teeth into while gently untwisting the precious center. Just thinking about its warm, pleasing aroma and distinctive taste lowers my blood pressure.

Dear Angelo died at age 96. Geez, when I knew him 45 years earlier, I thought he was old.

I still wonder if his "Lo, lo, lo" meant "Hello, hello, hello!" or whether he was announcing his name, "Angelo, Angelo, Angelo!" Either way, I'll bet the angels welcomed him in heaven with the same warm greeting he gave my neighborhood.

The Secret to Making the Best Pizzelle

I spent a snowy December morning making a batch of pizzelles while listening to Andrea Bocelli's Christmas CD. These anise-flavored Italian cookies are my Aunt Nee Nee's recipe. They're easy to make and look pretty on a Christmas plate.

Mix together:
6 eggs (room temperature)
1 cup vegetable oil
1 cup sugar
6 tsp baking powder
1 tsp vanilla
3 cups flour
3 TB anise seeds

Get your pizzelle iron hot. (If you haven't invested in a pizzelle iron, go buy one. It'll last forever.) Spray it with cooking spray. Use two teaspoons to drop a dollop of batter in the center of the pattern. If the first two cookies break or stick, don't be dismayed.

My mother used to make the batter while my father sat at the kitchen table operating the pizzelle iron. His secret for the perfect pizzelle? Lift the top after one quiet recitation of The

Lord's Prayer. Dad prayed a lot during Advent.

Lift the pizzelle from the iron with the edge of a sharp knife and rest on a baking rack until cooled. Then stack, serve, or gift wrap.

Mangia!

School Days

First Day of School Pictures

Every year on the first day of school, I'd pose my smiling daughters in front of the house in their new outfits with new backpacks and lunch bags. They were always eager to return to the classroom after summer vacation to meet their teacher and see friends.

So when my daughter Kristin, the newly minted elementary school teacher with her M.Ed., came downstairs one morning in her new first-day-of-school dress, I jokingly asked if she wanted me to take a picture.

"Mom, please," she said with a sigh.

She's worked hard for this moment. Her enthusiasm for young children is a joy to witness. Every parent wants an engaging and happy teacher like her.

My conscientious firstborn packed her tote bag and I wished her well. As she approached the door, she turned and asked, "Okay, do you want to take a picture? Because if you don't, you might regret it."

Aha! She loves the ritual as much as I do.

Teacher's Helper

When I was a kid, the last two weeks of summer couldn't pass quickly enough. While other kids soaked up their final hours of freedom on the beach or rode bikes, I itched to get back into the classroom.

"Can we go to Bond's now, Mom?" I'd ask enthusiastically.

Bond's was the variety store in town that sold school supplies. I loved inserting fresh looseleaf paper into a blue, three-ring binder along with subject dividers and a zippered pencil case that held #2 Ticonderogas, Bic pens, a small ruler, and a pink eraser.

So when my daughter asked me to help her set up her classroom in preparation for her first graders, I happily agreed. Colored bins! Scissors! Markers! Labels! Pocket folders! Magnets!

My first assignment was to create a word wall. I followed her instructions and used Velcro buttons to affix the laminated letters and words. Then she told me to organize the reading corner. Ah yes, another literary project. It took me three hours to sort hundreds of books. I categorized and labeled bins for: Animals, Science, Amelia Bedelia, Henry & Mudge, Dr. Seuss, Family, School & Learning, Sports, and more.

My daughter, the teacher, knows exactly how to motivate me.

Wit and Wisdom of Fifth Graders

On a summer visit to see Dad, I found his autograph book from grade school. He attended Girard School in Philadelphia and graduated fifth grade at age ten in June 1937.

We had fun reading the entries together and were impressed by the quality of penmanship. Dad remembered some of his Italian classmates: Caesar Monturano, Angelo Rollo, Gino Mastrostefano, Caroline Giannangelo, Katherine Alfonsi, Mary Primavera. Don't you love the sound of those names?

Here are a few messages we found amusing and prophetic.

Dear Amleto,
Labor for learning before you are old
For learning is better than silver and gold.
Silver and gold will tarnish away
But a good education will never decay.
—John A.

Dear Amleto,
When I get married and have a Ford
I'll let you sit on the running board.
Your Pal,
—Fiore Santoro

Air to air
Dust to dust
Give me a girl
That a boy can trust
—Richard Spagnuolo

Dear Amleto,
Down by the river
Curved on a rock
Are three little words
(forget me not)
Your classmate,
—Marie McIntyre

If wisdom's way you wisely seek
Five things observe with care
Of whom you speak
To whom you speak
And how, and when, and where.
—Jennie Murrow (teacher)

Second Grade Field Trip

Preparing for a field trip to the Franklin Mint, my second grade teacher, Mrs. Hayes, gave instructions on how she expected her students to behave.

Excitement quickly turned to disappointment when she announced that buddies would consist of a boy and a girl. To make matters worse, each boy got to choose which girl would be his partner. The sexual revolution hadn't started, but even at age seven I knew this was fundamentally wrong.

Mrs. Hayes started pairing us alphabetically in our suburban Philadelphia classroom. I noticed David Carroll sitting behind me in the row to my left, mouthing my name as he moved his clenched fists in circles around the desktop, waiting for his name to be called.

"David Carroll," Mrs. Hayes said in her Southern accent. "Whom do you choose as your partner?"

I turned around and saw chubby David grinning at me.

"Joyce Poggi," he said loudly.

I gave him a clumsy nod and swiveled back to face forward, relieved that I didn't have to sit through the whole alphabet of boys' name in order to be selected. David was a happy-go-lucky kid with blond hair, fair skin, and a perpetual smile. I could have done worse. Still, he was clearly more excited about the arrangement than I was.

Before boarding the bus the next day, Mrs. Hayes directed the boys to hold their partner's hands. I kept thinking: I shouldn't have to do this. It's not fair.

"We don't have to hold hands," I said while waiting in line. "I'm okay next to you."

"Mrs. Hayes says we have to hold hands!" he insisted. "It's the rule!" His fleshy, warm skin startled me.

Throughout the field trip, I'd drop my hand from his sweaty palm whenever possible. After all, my mother had taught me that occasionally it's okay not to follow the rules.

What I Learned in Wood Shop

While looking for the Christmas coffee mugs, I came across an old napkin holder in the back of a kitchen cabinet. I don't know why I've kept it all these years. My mother had delivered it to me as a vintage accent piece when I first became a homeowner, long after it had graced my family's kitchen table in the early 1970s.

In sixth grade, girls and boys switched classes for one week. Girls went to Industrial Arts (Shop) and boys went to Home Economics (Sewing). The teachers must have hoped there'd be a Maya Lin or Michael Kors among us.

While the boys threaded needles, girls learned how to use a saw, a hammer, and a plane to make wooden napkin holders. I remember using sandpaper to finish the top piece of the decorative napkin holder I deemed worthy of *Better Homes and Gardens*.

"Is this soft?" I politely asked the lanky, crabby shop teacher.

Mr. Woodshop took the piece of wood from my hand and hit me over the head with it.

"Does that feel soft to you?" he asked.

I stood there speechless, rubbing my head, wondering what I said that was so wrong.

"Smooth," he said. "Smooth, not soft. It's fine. Now go and pick out a stain color."

Who knew I'd get a vocabulary lesson in Industrial Arts?

Home from College

It's easy to tell when my daughter is home from college. She doesn't make a grand entrance nor does she raise her voice. She simply leaves her shoes, boots, and bags under the kitchen desk.

Half-empty water bottles are left around the house. She makes pancakes. The Nutella jar is emptier. There's an extra set of keys on the desk and another car in the driveway. She takes her seat next to me at the dinner table. She's the last one to bed at night and the last to wake up in the morning, always moving quietly. The sound machine on her nightstand remains on and ocean waves can be heard.

When she's away, the home feels unbalanced, like a table with a broken leg. When she comes home, balance is restored to the family.

I lie my head down at night, content. The house feels full. We are complete.

Favorite Teachers

I loved school. Everything about it. Well, almost everything. I loved looking at my roster taped to the inside cover of my three-ring denim binder in the seventh grade. I loved shuffling from classroom to classroom in junior high.

I loved listening to Miss Shalit talk about mythology. I loved how Mrs. Wysocki and Mrs. Eiseman kept me interested in science. I loved how Mr. Koshgerian engaged me in World Cultures and let me go to the blackboard. I loved Ms. Sassani's Women in Literature course and how she let me act out an Erma Bombeck skit for my presentation. I loved how Mrs. Turner fascinated me when discussing American literature and the transcendentalist movement. I loved Madame Bathish's enthusiasm for French.

(For the record, I detested gym class and couldn't understand Geometry to save my life.)

Then came college. I commuted to Villanova University and thought I'd hit the jackpot. I was so thrilled to be learning and engaging in meaningful discourse, especially in literature classes. I credit these inspiring teachers and most especially Villanova University for making me a lifelong learner.

Villanova Reunion: Touched by a Friend

One Friday night in October I met college friends for a reunion. All but one of our gang of eight girls attended. We were a clan of commuters who majored in the arts and lunched at the Pie Shop on the beautiful campus of Villanova University.

During the past thirty-four years, we pursued advanced degrees, married and bought homes, traveled, and put our children through college. We became successful women in business, education, and the law. We've suffered losses and now are taking care of our parents.

I became an outlier, settling in Massachusetts while they remained clustered in the Philadelphia suburbs. It was difficult for me to continue active friendships while they socialized and shared one another's personal milestones 350 miles away. Yet I never lost my affection for them.

We made lots of memories on campus, where a few of us worked part-time. After so many years, I don't remember details of classes and parties, but I do remember an incident that happened off-campus involving a friend named Carol. Every time I think of Carol or see her name, I recall one moment that transfixed me and solidified my respect for her.

She'd come to visit me with Peggy and Melinda while I was home sick with mono in the winter of sophomore year. We were sitting on my living room floor. With us was my brother, Jimmy, who is intellectually disabled. He was twenty at the time and his neighborhood friends had dispersed to begin independent lives. It was a difficult period for Jimmy because his formal education had ended and my parents were transitioning him to a new phase of life.

My friends gossiped about what I'd been missing. We were laughing, as was Jimmy, who was so eager to be a part of a group. Then Jimmy reached out and put his hand over Carol's hand. I drew in a breath, fearing Carol's reaction.

Carol left her hand there. She let my brother touch her. If she was startled or scared, she did not show it. She looked at me and then smiled at Jimmy and gave her signature, adorable laugh. He patted her hand another moment before removing it.

I spent four short years with Carol and thirty-four without her. Yet that single moment is the one I've never forgotten. It said everything to me about her character.

When Your First Love Dies

In memory of DWM
October 24, 1957–March 24, 1995

My mother rarely called me at work, so on that March morning in 1995 I suspected someone was sick. Her voice sounded different, calmer. Like a sad song, she said, "Joyce . . . De died," with heart-aching emphasis on De's name.

De was my first love, if that's what you call it at age nine. His real name was DeForrest, after his father, a prominent ob/gyn doctor. When a teacher would roll call the first time, De blushed while explaining his name. He corrected people when they called him Dean and he crossed out the second "e" when they wrote his name like a girl's.

We met in the fourth grade when I transferred to Drexel Hill Elementary. De had shiny, straight brown hair like mine, which I considered the key reason we made a cute couple. I figured if we married and had children, they could be models for Breck shampoo ads on the back cover of *Family Circle* magazine. De looked trendy wearing blue jeans cuffed at the bottom. He'd get in line behind me on the playground when the teacher blew the whistle to indicate recess ended. I could feel the heat of his body without him ever touching me. He might brush my arm in the hallway when we returned from art or music class. It was the closest I'd ever been to a boy, other than my brother, and I liked the new, tingling sensation when De came near me.

In the cafeteria I'd slide my tray along with my five-cent carton of milk and occasional block of butterscotch swirl ice cream, searching for De. He ate lunch at the same table every day with his crowd. He always sat in the corner seat facing my table of friends. We'd manage to lock eyes a few times before darting them back to our trays. After lunch, he kicked a soccer ball on the field with the boys while I played four square with the girls. For three years, De and I glanced at each other with uneven smiles.

When the school bell rang at three o'clock, sometimes he'd walk me home. I don't remember what De and I talked about on those afternoons, but we chatted more comfortably in the privacy of my yard than on the playground. Something about De's quiet and often serious demeanor made me want to be near him. When that happened, I felt breathless.

Although I yearned for De to kiss me, I refused to climb over the stone wall of the cemetery across the street and sit among tombstones with the fast kids playing Spin the Bottle. De never asked me to, but I had a hunch he would have played the game if I did. By the end of sixth grade, I wondered if De would still be interested in me when we entered junior high.

In the spring of 1969, before moving up to the junior high school, all the sixth-graders were swapping autograph books, a present from our teachers. The first entry in my dark-red book with flowers on the cover was from De. He wrote a verse: *"Roses are red, violets are blue, sugar is sweet, and so are you."*

Later that day, De asked for my book, insisting he wanted to write something else in it. A few moments later, he returned it, then scurried away without saying a word. I broke from the crowd on the playground, peeked inside the book and read what he added under his poem: "*I still like you. I like you more than anyone else does. Please don't drop me. I like you much too much.*"

Heat rose to my cheeks as I quickly closed the book before anyone could notice. De liked me a lot, maybe even more than I liked him. He recorded his intimate feelings about me. What did it mean? Where would it go? It wasn't just shy glances anymore. I tucked away my autograph book and resolved not to ask anyone else to sign it. No one except me would witness De's permanent expression of love.

Despite hopes from friends for a blooming romance, our preteen love fizzled during those apathetic early 1970s.

Then early in my sophomore year of college, I was pleasantly surprised to see De on campus. He had a careful, deliberate gait that crisp September day and approached me with a winsome smile. Handsome in his clean, dark-blue jeans that fit perfectly over his tall, thin frame, he held a stack of books against his hip. His shiny brown hair, soulful brown eyes, perfect teeth, and clean skin hinted of my first desire for him years earlier. Those features appeared more refined now. Soft-spoken, he explained how he decided to transfer to Villanova and was a commuter like me.

We didn't share any classes but bumped into each other on campus now and then. Although our preteen love never rekindled, we remained friendly for the next three years. Occasionally, he would offer me a ride to or from school in his silver Volkswagen Scirocco.

One night at the end of our senior year, during finals week, De drove me home from the college library where we had been studying.

"Thanks, De," I said as we approached my house, reaching for the car door handle. He startled me when he put his right hand on my left arm.

"Will you stay here with me a while?" he somberly asked.

"Uh, okay. Sure."

He turned off the ignition, then reached in his shirt pocket, lit up a joint, and offered it to me.

"No, thanks," I said, waving my hand at the smoke. I feared the odor getting on my clothes. My parents would have freaked out if they got a whiff.

On the half-hour ride home that moonlit night in early May, conversation had been easy. Sitting in the parked car, it seemed as if a melancholy wave washed over him. Was he worried about final exams? Where to go after graduation? Neither of us had firm plans.

"What's up, De?"

He shook his head then took another hit. I waited a moment before persisting.

"De, tell me. What's going on?"

Still no words.

"Come inside," I said.

"No, I can't."

"Why not?"

He stared out the windshield. It seemed as if an invisible shell closed around him.

"Come on, De," I said, nudging his shoulder, trying to cheer him. "Come inside and I'll make you a meatball sandwich."

"No," he answered softly. "Just stay here with me a little while longer, okay?"

We sat in silence a few minutes more until he finished the joint.

"Are you okay? You're going home now, right?" I pleaded, trying to make eye contact with him.

"Yeah, I'm fine," he said, avoiding my eyes.

"Okay. Goodnight. Thanks for the ride, De."

I paused before gathering my books, then hesitantly stepped out of the car. I closed the door gently and rested my hand on the door handle another moment. Then I bent down and looked at him through the window with a weak smile. Maybe he gave me one last shy smile or maybe he stared out the windshield. I don't remember.

That was the last time I saw De.

When my mother finished reading me the obituary from the *Philadelphia Inquirer*, I was still in shock. No cause of death was listed. De died at age thirty-seven. My jaw remained slack and a rainstorm gathered in the corners of my eyes. In slow motion, I hung up the phone, my sweaty palm momentarily stuck to the receiver. My shoulders shook as I dropped my head over my arms on the desk and sobbed.

The awkward images of our youth flashed before me. There stood De, an adorable, shy fourth-grader, head bowed, hands stuffed into the front pockets of his jeans, kicking pebbles between us in the schoolyard while trying to figure out what to say to me. Approaching my front porch. Pleading with me to write something else in my autograph book. In his high school soccer uniform. As the handsome, lanky, smart, introspective guy slipping between the socializing crowds on the campus green. And finally, in the car that night.

De graduated medical school and brought hundreds of lives into the world as an admired ob/gyn doctor in Atlanta, where no one knew his father's name. He never married or found someone special to create his own family. The note said he couldn't live with the pain any longer.

I wish I had put my arms around him that last night.

I hope I wrote something equally tender in his autograph book.

Namaste

Feel Good in Tree Pose

I discovered why I like tree pose so much after watching Amy Cuddy's famous TED Talk. The Harvard professor and researcher's video has been viewed more than 39 million times. If you haven't yet seen it, do yourself a favor and take the twenty minutes to watch it. If you've already seen it, it's worth watching again.

Cuddy discusses how our bodies can change our minds, our minds can change our behavior, and our behavior can change our outcomes. Opening up the body makes one feel powerful, optimistic, and confident.

So it's no wonder why every time I'm in tree pose (vrksasana) with my eyes on a focal point (drishti), the Helen Reddy song "I Am Woman" pops into my head. (I know . . . way back to 1971!) When that happens, I feel my best self and internally affirm as Ms. Reddy did: I am strong. I am invincible. Before long, I've held the pose and dispelled any self-doubt that might have previously lingered.

Try tree pose. If you're a beginner, place one foot on a stool or block to help balance yourself. If you can't raise your foot to your inner thigh, then modify by placing your foot on your calf. Just don't place your foot on the knee. Then raise your arms like tree branches reaching for the sky.

When you find yourself feeling down or anxious, do as

Cuddy suggests to lower your cortisol (the stress hormone): simply raise your arms in victory.

Intelligent Yoga Feet

We transitioned to standing poses halfway through yoga class. I stood in mountain pose (tadasana) when my instructor said something, quite seriously, that caused me to open my eyes.

"Your feet are becoming very intelligent." My classmates appeared equally impressed.

Intelligent feet? Who knew that creating space between my toes was a talent? I see bunions when looking at my feet—the lovely body feature inherited from my mother and grandmother. Those bunions ruined many leather pumps through the years. A friend once dubbed my dogs "refugee feet," pointing to the protruding veins and bones.

Several years ago, a sausage toe developed on the fourth toe of my left foot. That was the podiatrist's diagnosis. It turned out to be the first symptom of psoriatic arthritis. Other toes swelled and I suffered with Fred Flintstone feet for several weeks. My footwear was limited to loosely tied sneakers until I discovered the wonders of Mephisto and Naot sandals. Those shoes, meds, and an anti-inflammatory diet helped return my feet to glamorous metatarsals. My sister says now they look like rakes.

Finally, years after sausage toe and bony feet, someone complimented my feet, bunions and all. My size eight-and-a-half boats are intelligent enough to keep me balanced in bird of paradise and eagle poses for five to eight breaths. No wonder I favor the standing poses. I'm hoping my hands will develop equal amounts of intelligence so I can hold side crane longer.

Pursuit of a Headstand

After many attempts at headstand in yoga class, my right foot finally drew an invisible arc in the air, closely followed by my left foot drawing the same swoop. I was up! Whoo-hoo! In my mind, I heard a chorus of angels chanting a high-pitched "Ahhhhh."

Ten seconds later I brought my feet to the floor, then turned and smiled at my instructor, who gave me a thumbs up.

"I knew you could do it," she'd said. "You just had to believe in yourself."

My movements weren't always that graceful. When I started with beginner yoga classes, I found my quad muscles quickly. My triceps burned, hip joints ached, and wrists hurt. I couldn't balance on one foot for more than a few breaths. I wondered if I'd ever find the downward dog position restful.

Despite initial soreness and self-consciousness, I continued going to the studio. I learned yoga breathing—matching the length of each inhalation with the length of each exhalation. I felt better—nimble and lighter on my feet. I climbed stairs instead of taking the elevator, stood up straighter, lost a few pounds without trying, and felt an inner peace. I drove slower and wasn't agitated by waiting in line or in traffic.

Then at the end of that one class, Connie demonstrated headstand, the king of all poses.

"This is a restorative pose," she'd said. "It improves

circulation and generates new red blood cells. It also helps with the digestive and central nervous systems and has many other benefits."

I enviously watched her legs float up. My initial thought was, No way am I ever going to invert myself. It was too difficult and beyond my capability. I feared breaking my neck. Then I scanned the room and noticed women my age and older in headstand pose (sirsasana). They weren't the super-fit models in ads for yoga wear. These women resembled Connie and me and the average Jane who shops at the grocery store and pumps gas. If they can do it, I can do it.

With Connie's gentle encouragement, I gave it a try. Okay, let me begin against the wall. *Unh* . . . I groaned. I kicked one leg off the ground and it didn't go up very far. I tried again with the second foot, getting barely an inch off the yoga mat. Thud. My feet slammed the floor. My rear end felt as heavy as an anchor. Still, I remained undeterred. In every class for about a year, I inched, shimmied, hopped, kicked, and pushed. Up, up, thud. Up a little more, but not all the way.

Then the day finally came when I drew that invisible arc and turned myself upside down. And I've loved practicing headstand ever since.

When I close my eyes, I'm better able to focus on my breathing and hold the pose longer. While in headstand, I imagine all the organs of my body are given a little shake before settling into a new position. Now I can do a headstand in the middle of the room kicking up both feet together.

When my feet are weightless, directly above my head, I sense a feeling of freedom and think of nothing else but my breathing. Sometimes I recite prayers to myself. I swear that after inverting, my mind is clear of problems and ideas spew forth.

As my instructor often says, yoga is not about the pose or even holding the pose. It's what you learn about yourself in attempting to get into the pose. And that extends to what is learned off the mat. I learned that slowly, little by little, the impossible becomes possible.

To Pee or Not to Pee

While standing in eagle pose (garudasana) in a yoga class, I had a flashback to my six-year-old self on Stoneybrook Lane.

I used to tag along with my big sister, Lynne, and her friend Christine. They were in fifth and sixth grades and I thought they were the bee's knees. Their bodies were developing curves, they whispered secrets, played Monopoly, and were the bosses of neighborhood street games like Mother May I and Red Light/Green Light.

Whenever they played outdoors, I trailed them, carefully watching their every move so I'd know how to act grown up when I became their age. I didn't want to miss anything. If I had to pee, I'd cross my legs, wrap my foot around my calf, and squeeze.

"Joyce, go to the bathroom," Lynne would tell me.

"I don't have to go," I'd say, bouncing playfully, trying to hide my discomfort. There I was, a first-grader unknowingly practicing the eagle pose, standing on one foot, stooping lower and lower in the shade of our maple tree.

"Yes, you do," Christine would say, chuckling.

"Just go, Joyce," Lynne would say. "We'll be here when you get back."

With my bladder about to burst, I'd finally relent and rush indoors to the bathroom, wondering what I was missing. By the time I'd return to the front yard, they'd ditched me.

Shoveling to a Supported Backbend

Another Nor'easter and that means a cardio workout shoveling snow. While Mr. MOTM tackles the driveway with the snow blower, I clear the walkway and porch.

The storm dropped twenty inches of the white stuff. It was powder this time—much easier to throw than backbreaking wet snow.

I used to enjoy shoveling. Not so much anymore. Although I still love filling my lungs with cool New England air, this job is getting old. I pace myself and alternate left hand and right so as not to burden one side of my body.

A few shovels . . . straighten up. Throw more snow . . . rotate head, massage neck, and gaze at the blue sky. Look across the street . . . why isn't Ellen out yet?

After peeling off the layers and hanging them on a wooden rack to dry, I settle into a supported backbend pose. This is a fantastic way to relax after doing anything where you're hunched over with rounded shoulders such as shoveling, gardening, lifting toddlers, driving, or sorting laundry.

Lie down on the floor and place one foam or cork block lengthwise across your back, just under the tips of your shoulders. (For women, position it where your bra strap would be.) Place a second block under your head at whatever level feels comfortable. Keep your palms up. This is a great heart opener. Namaste.

How Vinyasa Improved My Golf Swing

Mr. MOTM and I met friends for a round of golf. We've known one another for more than twenty years, so I knew they'd be patient with my lack of talent on the fairway. Still, since they play regularly, I announced a disclaimer before we started the nine holes.

As a perennial beginner, I generally stick with the three wood, seven iron, pitching wedge, and putter. Whenever I get to the links, I ask myself why I don't play more often. It's a great game and meets my specs as a non-athlete: no physical contact with others, not too much sweating, and a beautiful atmosphere. You really don't think about anything else except getting that ball in the hole.

I recalled golf lessons from years ago, when an instructor told me to take my time with the back swing. Then my yoga practice came to mind. When transitioning from upward dog (urdhva mukha svanasana) to down dog (adho mukha svanasana), I used to move swiftly.

A few months ago, I altered the movement to a slower, deliberate transition to down dog. In doing so, I discovered a more thoughtful, fluid experience. Envisioning the vinyasa (synchronizing breath and movement in a flowing format) while addressing the ball helped with my stroke and follow-through.

With that in mind, my golf game that day wasn't a total embarrassment. A couple of bogeys and some nice putts. I'm still far from par but, as with yoga practice:

> *"Slowly, slowly. Little by little.*
> *Practice and all is coming."*
> —Sri Krishna

Yoga in the Dentist's Chair

My sister Alison has logged more hours in the dentist's chair than anyone I know. So naturally she was the first person I called when my dentist informed me I needed a root canal.

"I'm scared."

"Are you in pain?" Alison asked.

"No. It's just very sensitive, especially to cold."

"You'll be okay. Get it done now."

"Is it going to hurt?"

"Nah. The reason root canal gets a bad rap is because people wait too long, until they're in real pain, before going to the dentist. Sounds like you're ahead of the pain. Just get it over with."

My family doesn't coddle. I can always count on Alison to give it to me straight. Once, I told her I thought I had the beginning of a urinary tract infection. Her response? "Get to the doctor now before it feels like you're peeing razor blades."

Back to my teeth. I booked an appointment with the endodontist and bravely sat in the chair for two hours. When the clacking of metal instruments began, I closed my eyes and started breathing slowly and mindfully, matching the length of each inhale to the length of each exhale.

"Are you all right?" asked the endodontist. With my mouth expanded like a sinkhole, I gave him a thumbs-up sign.

"Is that yoga breathing you're doing?" he asked.

Another thumbs up.

Perhaps I got to the endodontist before experiencing acute pain, but the yoga breathing helped me forget the buzzing of the drill and my anxiety of root canal.

I called Alison immediately after leaving the office.

"It wasn't as bad as I thought."

"See?" she said. "Told ya."

If you're experiencing anxiety about going to the dentist or anywhere unpleasant, turn on yoga breathing (ujjayi). It'll get you through the day.

Handstand to Hospital

An hour after yoga class, I was sitting at my desk when a stabbing pain hit me in the center of my chest, right between the ribs. *Yowza! What the heck was that?* Another jolt. I got up from the desk and walked around the house, massaging my sternum, trying to shake it off. I even drove to the store to distract myself, which seemed to help a bit. Even though I consider myself to be in good health, I'd read enough articles about women ignoring the signs of a heart attack, often dismissing them as indigestion.

Three hours later, the stabbing pain persisted and at more frequent intervals. I felt pins and needles in my fingers and couldn't catch my breath. I called hubby, who said he'd drive me to the hospital. When I hung up the phone, I realized I couldn't wait the twenty minutes it would take him to get home. In the bedroom, doubled over, wincing in pain, clutching my midsection, I called 911.

The paramedics arrived before hubby (who later told me he thought I could have been dead when he saw the ambulance in the driveway). For the second time in my life, I was carried out of the house in a stretcher, this time in the January cold, versus last time in the June sun. I recoiled at every bump in the road on the way to the hospital.

Once in the ER, I was given a dose of morphine. A

variety of medical professionals traipsed in and out of the room, asking the same questions, poking and prodding me. Tests, X-rays, blood draws, echocardiogram, more tests.

"I'm really a healthy person," I said, trying to convince the staff as much as myself.

"Let's monitor you overnight," said the doctor. After being subjected to all the pinging and rattling in the ER for five hours, I was relieved to be moved to a quiet room. That is until I met my roommate, an eighty-eight-year-old incontinent woman who moaned incessantly.

"Please move me to another room or I'll never pass the stress test tomorrow," I said to the nurse.

When all the test results showed my heart and other organs were functioning normally, the doctors concluded that the cause of the pain was muscle spasms. Specifically, my rectus abdominis was working overtime. That's the muscle group in the center of your torso between the ribs. I figured it happened while practicing handstand (adho mukha vrksasana) in yoga class. That morning had been the first time in two years I'd completed the challenging pose.

It took another eight months until I summoned the courage and developed a stronger core to attempt handstand again.

Yoga on the Beach

Hubby and I took a midweek getaway to Cape Cod. We wanted to avoid weekend traffic and arrive before schools let out for summer vacation.

I woke early to attend a sunrise yoga class on the beach at Chatham Lighthouse. Fourteen other people joined me as we faced the ocean shortly after dawn and followed our instructor's lead.

A gentle breeze, the cool sand underfoot, and the smell of salt air filled me up. My singular view was the natural stripes of an azure sky, the deep-blue ocean reflecting morning sun, grassy dunes, and a tan, sandy beach—all my favorite soothing colors. Now and then a tern soared across my line of vision. The only sound I heard while practicing was an occasional ripple at the water's edge.

This yoga session gave a whole new meaning to sun salutation.

Sun Salutation to Sleep

Through the years I've used different strategies to combat insomnia: watching late-night TV (especially *House Hunters International*), reading, repeating the Lord's Prayer, counting backward from ninety-nine, sipping wine or chamomile tea. Depending on what's worrying me, some or none of these techniques work.

In late 2012, I experienced sleepless nights fretting about my father's displacement due to Hurricane Sandy. Was he lonely or scared? Was he safe? Was he eating well? When would the contractors be done? I'd fixate on his unfortunate situation and then mentally itemize my to-do list for the following day to help him through the ordeal.

Around the same time I joined a new yoga studio. It's an oasis of calm, with instructors who are precise, encouraging, and nonjudgmental. No matter how my practice goes, when I leave the studio, I feel strong and clear-headed.

On one of those restless nights, I lay in corpse pose (savasana) and imagined myself in the studio practicing one sun salutation after another. I only recognized the result of peaceful sleep when I awoke the following morning feeling restored.

My daughters tell me I worry too much. They're right. I remind them it's one of the things I do best, tending to fast forward to disaster. Worry will always be there, especially in the darkness of night, when everything seems magnified. However, this method for dealing with insomnia is working for me. Maybe it'll work for you, too.

(By the way, my father returned to his home safe and sound seven weeks after the hurricane.)

Traveling
AROUND

A Chartreuse Sky

I looked out the window and suddenly caught myself smiling and humming "Here Comes the Sun," by the Beatles.

At 6:20 a.m., on a flight to Barcelona, I spotted a glow in the distance. Seconds later, an orange speck appeared. The marmalade dot widened and brightened. I grabbed my iPhone but couldn't effectively capture the image. So I took out my notepad to remember the majestic sight with words instead of a photo.

Here comes the sun . . .

I kept moving my gaze above and below the plane's wing as a spectacle of color emerged between a blue gray swath and cotton-ball clouds.

Here comes the sun . . .

Soon I witnessed Impressionism unlike any piece of famous artwork. Shades of blue, green, yellow, and pink emerged. Even a chartreuse layer blurred the horizon.

Here comes the sun . . .

The blinding orange ball forced me to look away. Spots floated in front of my eyes, making it difficult to scribble notes on the page, but I persisted. I turned to my daughter seated next to me, ready to rouse her from sleep, but stopped short when I noticed the amber glow on her face.

Little darling
The smiles returning to the faces
Little darling
It seems like years since it's been here
Here comes the sun
Here comes the sun, and I say
It's all right.

The Old Station Wagon

In the spring of 1979, while I was fretting about finding a job after college graduation, four of my friends were planning a cross-country trip. They reasoned that the start of forty years of employment could be delayed by a few months in order to witness the majestic beauty of our U S of A.

So when Peggy and Nick and Carol and Bob said they needed to buy a car for their trip of a lifetime, I suggested my parents' station wagon: a 1971 Country Squire with 67,000 miles on it. My pals paid 500 dollars for the car and:

Drove 10,535 miles
Across 8 major rivers
Into 26 states
Visiting 11 state capitals
And 8 national parks
Sleeping in multiple campgrounds
And 8 hotels
In 50 days (May 29 to July 17)

1979 was the summer of the gas crisis. Some states had the odd/even rule, designating when you could tank up. The lowest price the sightseers paid for gas was seventy-three cents per gallon in Texas.

The fearless foursome took good care of the old wagon. Peggy and Carol straightened out the back of the car every morning, arranging suitcases, coolers, and camping gear for the next leg of their journey.

Nick, the engineer, was in charge of all things mechanical and did a thorough job of maintaining the car fluids and filters, etc. At one point, the station wagon wasn't shifting properly. A guy in South Dakota determined the problem to be a crack in the vacuum hose. He fixed it and told my friends they didn't owe him anything, but of course they paid him for his service.

Thirty-seven years later, the spirited group still reminisces about their expedition in the trusty Country Squire station wagon. They have more memories of their fifty days driving that prized vehicle than my family does for the eight years we owned it.

So whatever happened to the classic wagon? Upon returning home, the vacationers cleaned and waxed it and sold it for the same 500 dollars. Three years later, Peggy and Nick married. They haven't stopped traveling since.

A Friendly Walk

Almost, ready, Ellen? I ask my friend who lives across the street.

Be right there, Joyce, she answers while tying the laces of her sneakers.

Colder out than I thought.

Damp, too, she says as we begin our morning walk.

Ellen, are you warm enough with just that fleece vest on?

Feels warm enough for me.

Geez, I've got three layers on.

How's your Dad? she asks.

I think he's on the mend now, thank goodness, and how's your Dad?

January was a difficult month for him but he's hanging in there.

Kelly house had new windows installed, did you see? I ask, pointing.

Looks like they went for the craftsman style.

Makes the house looks brighter.

Notice the Dumpster at the green house on Barrows Lane? says Ellen.

Only yesterday I saw an electrical contractor truck there, I say.

Physicians live in that house, right?

Quacks, from what I hear.

Really?

Sandy told me.

Town gossip, she is.

Usually she's right though.

Valentine's Day is coming up, says Ellen.

What are you getting for Bob?

X-rated chocolates.

You're kidding me!

Zip-a-dee-doo-dah! she sings with a bounce in her step.

Farewell, Four-Wheeled Friend

Goodbye, Madeline. After 129,000 miles, I'm trading you in for a newer version of yourself: a 2016 Acura MDX. She's white with beige interior, just like you.

You were a loyal and reliable friend. Until we met, I'd never kept someone like you for as long as ten years. You took me back and forth to Long Beach Island, New Jersey, on all those lonely six-hour excursions to visit Dad.

You protected me from the aggressive eighteen-wheelers on Route 84, the narrow stretches of the Garden State Parkway, and the never-ending construction on the Tappan Zee Bridge. During some of those trips, you listened to me weep with worry and sing off key.

We traveled throughout New England together, visiting beaches, ski resorts, and coastal towns. We picked up friends and family at the airport. I packed you with my daughters' college dorm gear.

I filled you with sand chairs, a beach umbrella, golf clubs, yard sale finds, luggage, and many bags from HomeGoods and T.J.Maxx.

Our predictable routes around town found us at the yoga studio, the library, CVS pharmacy pick-up, and the market.

I did my best to keep you tidy, giving you regular baths, oil changes, and tune-ups. You got four new rubber shoes twice in our time together. You never complained when I dropped cracker crumbs on the seat or sloshed dirty snow on the all-weather mats.

I hope you don't mind that I'm transferring a few things from you to my new friend: an umbrella, ice scraper, beach blanket, and the Villanova University Alumni license plate holder.

Thanks for the memories, Madeline.

Searching for Imperfections

Nothing beats a walk on the beach to clear your head. Any beach. Any time of year. Sauntering, walking briskly, or in running shoes. When hubby and I vacationed on lovely Marco Island, Florida, I paused on our morning strolls to collect shells unique to the Gulf Coast.

Marco Island shells are tiny compared to the ones I find on the beaches of Long Beach Island, New Jersey, and in New England.

I found myself tossing or passing miniature whelks and scallops that were damaged. On the third day, I realized I wanted some of those imperfect shells. They tell a story of being tossed by the beautiful, dangerous sea.

I thought of my own imperfections: the broken blood vessel that's a pink dot on the bridge of my nose, the scar on my middle finger that I got opening a can of orange juice in my youth, my bunions. I enjoy collecting shells and stones from various vacation spots, preferring to bring home a piece of the earth rather than a T-shirt.

Imperfections of shells and sea glass add to the beauty of collections.

Boston's Garden of Remembrance

"Time touches all more gently here . . ."

One of my favorite places in Boston is the Public Garden. It's lush with botanicals, colorful flowers, and exotic trees. A lagoon, a footbridge, fountains, and statues attract you while strolling the winding paths.

When entering from the Arlington Street gate, be sure to take a right before approaching the equestrian statue of George Washington. There you will find Boston's Garden of Remembrance. The pink granite memorial honors the more than 200 individuals with ties to Massachusetts who died in the 9/11 attacks.

Never forget.

Goodbye, Summer

(To be sung to the tune of "My Favorite Things" from The Sound of Music. LBI is Long Beach Island, an eighteen-mile-long barrier island in New Jersey.)

Sundrops on my toes and whistles on lifeguards
Bright colored beach kites and twinkling evening stars
Walks on the beach with a fun friend who sings
These are a few favorite LBI things.

Smell of salt water and ice cream with sprinkles
Sea glass and sand chairs and beach towels with wrinkles
Sandpipers searching for what tourists bring
These are a few favorite LBI things.

Children in flip-flops with sand toys they're towing
Sea breeze that keeps my skin pink and a-glowing
Silvery waters and young kids on swings
These are a few favorite LBI things.

When the gull swoops
When the bee stings
When I feel a burn
I simply remember my LBI things
And then I plan to return.

Just
FOR FUN

The Weekend I Didn't Get Engaged

I had booked a trip to the romantic island of Nantucket on Labor Day weekend. My boyfriend (with whom I'd been living at the time) and I planned to ride our bikes onto the ferry and travel light. He'd carry the larger backpack with a metal frame and I'd carry the smaller pack with our incidentals.

The night before leaving, he stood at the foot of the bed rolling T-shirts and shorts while I collected toiletries in the bathroom. I surveyed his bulky travel case on the counter, then my slimmer kit, and decided it would be more efficient to combine our toiletries and bring one bath case. I'd never touched his travel kit, wallet, or briefcase. However, sharing shampoo and toothpaste on a weekend trip to an island seemed like the most economical thing to do at the time.

Unzipping his black bag, I called out, "I'm putting your toiletries in my case so we only have to carry one." With the words barely out of my mouth and the zipper opened, my eyes locked onto a small white bag with a jeweler's name on it. A quiet gasp stuck at the back of my throat. Guilt and glee overtook me and I couldn't contain a smile. Without a chance to close the zipper, he appeared in the doorway. He paused for a second and then yelled, "You ruin everything!"

I looked at him and froze. I had to suppress a giggle but felt sorry for ruining his surprise. A *grrrr* of disgust emerged from between his teeth and he stomped his foot for emphasis. Then he grabbed his bath kit and stormed off.

A few weeks earlier, we had gone to the jewelers' building in Boston. He asked me to select the style of engagement ring I wanted. I felt confident he'd buy the brilliant cut, one-carat stone with a smaller stone on each side set in a yellow gold band. All I had to do was wait and soon enough he'd pop the question.

I wanted to jump for joy and tell someone the impending good news but feared bad luck if I announced fiancée status prematurely. So I packed my own bath kit and disappeared downstairs with nail polish and gave myself a manicure. While perfecting each nail, I wiggled in the chair with joy. When and where would he propose? How would I react? Would he be on bended knee? Surely he planned a romantic setting somewhere on the island.

We didn't speak for the rest of the night. We had to rise early the next day to catch the ferry, yet I couldn't sleep, imagining a beautiful engagement scene that I had dreamed about for so long.

After showering the next morning, I felt light on my feet and tried to suppress a grin. He gave me his bath case to pack in my bag, so I presumed he removed the ring and stashed it somewhere else. Would he still propose this weekend? My breathing remained shallow as he kept me in suspense. We rode our bikes along a scenic path to the ferry and settled in for the two-hour boat trip to Nantucket.

As I unpacked our bags in the quaint B&B, I noticed him reach for his case. Instead of leaving it unzipped on the bathroom counter, he kept it zipped and stored on a shelf in the closet. Clearly, he hadn't hidden the engagement ring somewhere else, nor had he left it home. Hope sprung! I'd lose my single status soon.

Each time we'd get ready to leave the inn, I'd spy his movements to see if he might have retrieved a small box. I'd check his pockets to see if they lay flat or bulged with a ring box. All weekend long I waited for the moment women dream about—for the love of my life to ask me to marry him. I selected pretty outfits, reapplied lipstick, and practically posed at every opportune venue. While we window-shopped along the cobblestone streets, I soaked in the island beauty, trying to distract myself. I tried to capture every image so I could hold it indelibly in my mind. I kept glancing at my left hand imagining the diamond that would soon adorn it. Meanwhile, he moseyed along, undisturbed.

The request for my hand in marriage didn't happen after we bicycled to 'Sconset. It didn't happen at dusk on the beach in Madaket. It didn't happen downtown on the park bench overlooking the harbor. I felt certain it would happen after Saturday night's candlelight dinner. It didn't. I sunk into myself, becoming emotionally deflated after every island adventure.

While waiting for the ferry to go home, I could barely break a smile or look at him. We'd had an otherwise fun weekend exploring the island on bicycle and foot, dining, shopping, and sunning ourselves on pristine beaches. Although I'd been living with him for two years and felt a commitment without being married, I wondered now if he was having second thoughts about our relationship. Was he punishing me? Would he still propose and, if so, when? I became angry at myself for taking the wind out of his sail and ruining what should have been a memorable weekend.

Ironically, I carried that ring in my backpack onto the island and all the way back home. While unpacking, I said, "Well, you might as well wait until my birthday," which fell in early November. My sister was getting married in mid-October and I didn't want to show up at her wedding with an engagement ring on my finger and steal her thunder.

On my birthday, he booked dinner at a favorite Italian restaurant. I polished my nails and dressed up for the occasion. Before leaving the house, he presented me with a bouquet of red roses. Now? I thought. No. Off we went to dinner where the maître d' seated us at a secluded table.

Dinner started with wine and a toast to us. Now? I wondered. No. I skipped an appetizer and we waited for our entrees. Now? No. Dear Lord, he was making me sweat. Could he possibly not ask me to marry him? We finished our meals and ordered coffee and dessert. A pause. Finally, he reached into his suit jacket and instead of pulling out his wallet, he retrieved a small black velvet box. He opened it and, with a smile, asked, "Will you marry me?"

He had bought the ring I wanted. Although it wasn't presented to me in the romantic setting on Nantucket that he planned, he still made the moment special at a table dubbed "the engagement corner." I've worn the sparkler every day for the last twenty-five years of our happy marriage.

So You Didn't Win the Powerball Lottery

Now you don't have to spend time thinking about which Fiji island to buy, where to park the matching Rolls Royces, or hiring someone to pilot your Lear jet.

You don't have to hire a financial advisor, accountant, lawyer, estate planner, or bodyguard.

There's no need to change your phone number to fend off all your new "friends," decide which charities to donate to, or feel compelled to pick up the tab for customers in line with you at Target or your favorite coffee shop.

You needn't decide how much money to give to family members, what sum to donate to your alma mater, or what type of campus building you want erected with your name on it.

You needn't decide which hungry real estate agent will list your house, or who you want to find your new penthouse suite, Italian villa, ranch, ski lodge, and beachfront home.

You don't have to revise your will, change the locks on your doors, install a home security system, or worry about whom to trust.

Remember Kino, the poor fisherman in John Steinbeck's novel *The Pearl*? It didn't take him long to realize the curse of finding the rare and valuable gem.

Hips Don't Lie

Not the alarm. Not birds chirping or the smell of coffee brewing stirs me in the morning. Before raindrops ping the bedroom windows, before the street becomes wet and slick, before the delivery guy tosses the newspaper in the driveway, I know it's about to rain.

I feel a dull ache on my left hip. I turn over. The clock reads 4:00 a.m. My right hip is equally sore so I rest on my back.

How is it that I can snuggle under three layers of bedding in a warm home and yet my bones can detect the outdoor humidity? What's the science there?

While descending the stairs more slowly than usual, I hear the singer Wyclef Jean calling, "Shakira, Shakira!" in the classic sexy video.

Sadly, the only thing I have in common with the beautiful and talented Shakira, for obviously different reasons, is that "my hips don't lie."

Is That a Cat?

My friend Ellen and I enjoy our morning walks together. We talk about our family and our town and like to see what changes people make to their homes and gardens.

One Sunday, we rounded a bend on the last 100 yards to our houses (Ellen lives directly across the street from me), when I interrupted her story to make an observation.

"Ellen, look, there's a turkey." It dashed across the front lawn of the house about twenty-five yards from us. We've seen our share of wild turkey strutting around and even been awakened by their squawking.

"Oh, but what's that?" she said, stopping short.

"What?"

"There. Between the two rocks," she pointed. "See it?"

I saw a thick, dark tail and the back half of an animal that remained still.

"Uh oh," I said, taking a step back. I felt my heartbeat quicken. "I don't know, but I don't think it's a cat."

"It must be a fisher cat!" said Ellen, who started flailing her arms.

"Ellen, stay still," I said, pivoting carefully. I glanced back and saw a face between those two rocks, staring menacingly at me.

I heard there'd been fisher cats that came down the wooded

hill behind the homes on that side of the street but had never seen one. We figured this creature was chasing the turkey as prey.

"Okay," I said, trying to remain calm. "Let's go to the Coughlin house."

"No," she said. "Let's go over here and cut through the back yards 'til we get to your house."

I debated climbing the stairs to the deck of a new neighbor to seek shelter. Hi. Welcome to the neighborhood. I know we haven't met yet but can I come in because there's a wild critter across the street and I'm scared to death.

"Should we knock on the back door here?"

"No!" said Ellen. "Just keep walking."

I led the way through some bushes, only looking straight ahead. I was afraid that if I made eye contact with the feral quadruped, it would charge me.

Ellen and I nervously laughed while hyperventilating as we kept a quick stride.

"Come to my house," I said. Hers is situated two houses down from the sighting.

"No, thanks. I'm going home," she said, "but watch me until I get inside." She skittered up the driveway and entered through the side door while I stood guard by my garage.

Once safely inside, I breathed a sigh of relief and then Googled fisher cats. The image didn't match what I witnessed, so I called her.

"Ellen, I saw pointed ears. Do you think it was a coyote?"

"No, I think it was some kind of cat. Look up bobcat," she said.

We agreed the critter was a bobcat. We've added it to our list of animal sightings, along with deer, cows, cats, dogs who sometimes follow us, Canada geese, owls, dead mice on the road, and garter snakes. Raccoons, fisher cats, coyote, and fox have been spotted by neighbors at night. Thankfully, we haven't come upon them during our morning walks.

I'm Ready!

One Friday night, after the pizza plates were cleared away, I sat in my sweats, strumming my fingers on the kitchen table, eager to start a game of Yahtzee.

"I'm ready," I sang out to my husband, who was taking too long in the bathroom.

When he emerged, he said flatly, "You know, there was a time when you used to say 'I'm ready' the same way. Only I'd find you posed in bed in something sexy."

Part-Time Jobs

Parents tell their teenage kids that part-time jobs build character. They learn discipline, teamwork, and how to take direction from others. Here are some of my memorable gigs.

Camp counselor—age 14. Seems like all I did was tie the shoelaces and wipe the noses of five-year-old boys.

Pharmacy cashier—age 15. After stocking the candy shelves, I'd snack on Peanut Chews and Baby Ruth bars behind the register.

Telephone surveyor—age 16. In a room of ten cubicles, I called homeowners and questioned them about their use of the Yellow Pages.

Sales clerk at Hit or Miss (discount retailer)—age 17. Lots of hanging, folding, and cleaning out dressing rooms. I liked using the little contraption that attached a price tag into the seam of a garment.

Insurance clerk—age 17. The summer before entering college, I worked at State Farm typing, folding claims and invoices, and stuffing envelopes.

Library employee—age 18. I worked at the circulation desk of the Villanova University library. For a few weeks one summer, I worked side by side with an Indian seminarian, affixing bar code labels to the inside cover of books. He taught me about a language called Urdu.

The Stillness of Summer

Humidity hangs in the air on my morning walk.
No breeze.
Few cars drive through in the neighborhood.
No strollers or kids on bikes.
Several newspapers lie at the end of a driveway.
Families vacation at beaches and lakes.
No dog walkers. No barking.
The only sound is the clang of a painter's ladder.
I remove my hat and wipe my sweaty hairline.
Only two blooms on the hydrangea bush.
The grass crunches like straw underfoot.
White-gray clouds move slowly across the sky.
When will the rain come?

Where Do You Sit?

I made it to yoga class early to claim my favorite spot: second row by the wall, close to the lobby door. I like that spot. It gives me some privacy, and when I look up while in a pose, there's no pot light above to hurt my eyes.

As I rolled out my mat, it occurred to me how I'd pick a similar spot whenever entering a new classroom in high school and college. I never wanted to sit in the first seat like a goody two-shoes nor did I want to hang in the back with the boys who disrupted class. I wanted a respectable distance from the teacher, enough to let her know I was eager to learn. With a wall on one side of me, I had a decent view of the entire classroom.

Even when attending business meetings, I'd select a seat on the end and close to the door of a conference room. Same goes for church—I choose to sit in a pew on the side section of church near the aisle instead of the center. It's important for me to exit a large room quickly in case of emergency, particularly since I'm not a fan of crowds.

Some people enjoy being in the middle of the action. I'm comfortable on the periphery, with a long view.

These Boots Are Made for ... Everything

I spent several hours raking on Saturday. I didn't mind because the fall weather was crisp and I was wearing my favorite boots. These babies are named Herman Survivors for good reason. They've lasted twenty-eight years and I have no intention of replacing them.

Mr. MOTM bought the indestructible footwear for me one Christmas before we married. Aiming to introduce his indoor girl to the great outdoors, he couldn't have known how much I'd love these boots or that they'd rank as one of my favorite gifts.

I've worn my Herman Survivors hiking in the White Mountains of New Hampshire during fall foliage season, in ski lodges throughout New England, sledding with the kids, and to the local playground. I've laced them up and plodded between bushes to rake leaves, to clean the garage, to garden, to sweep outdoors, to move furniture, you name it. When they were new (and I, much younger), I even wore them with fashionable leggings and a tunic top to work one casual Friday to the bemused stares of a few software engineers.

I don't know what it is about these boots, but I've always felt strong and confident wearing them. They've never let me down in any season. Worn with only a single pair of raglan socks, they've kept my feet warm and dry even in the slushiest of New

England's stormy winters. These waffle stompers have kept me steady on my feet and prevented mosquitoes from biting my ankles while planting and weeding.

Whether I'm slipping them on or slipping them off, my bodily sensation is always *ahhh*.

Women's Winning Suits

I watched women's beach volleyball on TV all weekend. The athleticism of those women amazes me. Their speed and agility. Their strength and determination. And how about their muscles? If only I could have rock-hard abs. What amazes me more than all that, though, is how their teeny, weeny bikini bottoms stay on. Admit it, you can't take your eyes off their tushes.

Yet the athletes remain laser-focused on their job and couldn't care less if the swatch of fabric sized for a Barbie doll rides up a cheek or gets stuck . . . well, you know where.

I haven't worn a bikini in ages. Yet when wearing my one-piece bathing suit, I can't stand how the elastic feels as tight as a vacuum cleaner belt digging in to the tops of my thighs. Add sand to the equation and it can get uncomfortable just sitting in my beach chair. Imagine diving for a volleyball under the beating sun and coating yourself in sand like a chicken cutlet in bread crumbs. Give me the clicker and a comfy chair. I'm a better spectator than athlete.

I love to see women competing, succeeding, and winning at any pursuit: an athletic competition, business, medicine, academia, yoga, the arts. To see years of education, training, strategy, and teamwork result in success leaves me in awe.

Some people find the women's beach volleyball uniforms

offensive. It doesn't matter to me if a woman wears a bikini, a business suit, or scrubs. If she's working hard at her craft, then I'm rooting for her and she's a winner in my book.

You Don't Ask, You Don't Get

My daughter took a favorite necklace to the jeweler for repair. Two months had passed while she worked full-time at a summer internship before realizing she still hadn't received a call from the jeweler. She finally found time to reclaim the necklace just before returning to college for her senior year.

"Since it took so long, do I still have to pay the full amount?" she asked the sales associate.

"Yeah, you still do, sweetie."

"Thought I'd ask."

"You could have called," admonished the woman.

"That's your job," answered my daughter, cool as a cucumber. "I think consideration should be made for the fact that I was never informed the necklace was ready."

Realizing my daughter was no pushover, the sales associate called her manager over to the glass display case and relayed the problem.

"Well, the service was done," said the manager.

"The repair was done," asserted my daughter, matter-of-factly. "The service isn't complete until the customer is called."

The sales associate bristled. The manager paused and offered, "Okay. You can either pay half or pay the full amount."

"Since I have to buy textbooks next week, I'll pay half."

I'm glad to know my daughter is applying the life lesson of "You don't ask, you don't get."

Favorite Time of the Week

My favorite time of the week is late Sunday afternoon when I sit on the screened porch and settle down with the Boston Globe Sunday crossword puzzle and Sudoku. There's usually a breeze and the neighborhood is quiet but for a few birds chirping. Mr. MOTM reads the paper nearby and we enjoy a glass of wine with some veggies and hummus. A golf tournament on TV adds to the relaxing mood.

What's your favorite time of the week?

Acknowledgments

Thank you to the readers of my blog, especially those who posted comments and encouraged me to keep writing.

Thank you to my writing partner, Kathleen Molloy Nollet.

Thank you Amy Marcott, Deborah Sosin, and Kelly Pelissier.

Thank you Kristin Olson and the community of Home Yoga.

Thank you Lynne, Jimmy, and Alison for your inspiration.

Thank you Gary, Kristin, and Melissa for your love and support.

Visit Joyce's website at:
www.joycepoggihager.com

Made in the USA
Columbia, SC
04 June 2018

Musing
OFF THE MAT

memories & everyday moments

Joyce Poggi Hager

Musing Off the Mat
Copyright © 2017 by Joyce Poggi Hager